Pouring New Wine
Into
Old Wineskins

By Aubrey Malphurs

Developing a Vision for Ministry in the Twenty-first Century
Planting Growing Churches for the Twenty-first Century

Pouring New Wine
Into
Old Wineskins

*How to Change a Church
Without Destroying It*

Aubrey Malphurs

Foreword by Leith Anderson

A Division of Baker Book House Co.
Grand Rapids, Michigan 49516

© 1993 by Aubrey Malphurs

Published by Baker Books
a division of Baker Book House Company
P.O. Box 6287, Grand Rapids, MI 49516-6287

Second printing, July 1994

Printed in the United States of America

Library of Congress Cataloging-in-Publication Data

Malphurs, Aubrey.
    Pouring new wine into old wineskins : how to change a church without destroying it / Aubrey Malphurs : foreword by Leith Anderson.
        p.   cm.
    Includes bibliographical references and index.
    ISBN 0-8010-6301-9
    1. Church   management.   2. Church   renewal.   3. Change—Religious aspects—Christianity.   I. Title.
    BV652.M3564   1993
    254—dc20   93-10368

To all those leaders who have dared
to color outside the lines in traditional situations,
especially those from Dallas Seminary
such as Randy Frasee, Andrew McQuitty,
and many others.

Contents

Contents

Foreword

When *Changing Times* magazine changed its name to *Kiplinger Personal Finance,* I realized that even the changes were changing.

Changes are cascading around us with hurricane force. The newspapers and television reports can no longer keep up, and most of us have long ago given up trying to read everything in the newspaper or watch everything on television. We may want to withdraw to some safe haven where change will never invade and yesterday will live forever.

Can the church be our safe haven from change? Hardly! The church is no more exempt from change than business, school, family, or government. Like it or not, the church is in the world, and the world is changing.

Our choices are few. We can pretend changes aren't happening. We can build walls to keep changes away. Or we can open all the doors and windows and be changed by the changes. None of these are wise or practical. The best choice is to deal with change from a biblical base, incorporating the best and excluding the worst.

There is great hope for the future. Thousands of Christians and churches are following the pattern of the descendants of Issachar who "understood the times and knew what to do." In their case it was the change from the reign of Saul to the reign of David. Today it is from the old paradigms for "doing church" to the new paradigms for "doing church."

Neither the issues nor the changes are limited to individual leaders or isolated churches. The challenges facing us are everywhere. The success and survival of the church is at stake. It is not a matter of a single sick church or a misfit pastor. Changes are necessary in the entire system.

Surely there is resistance. There always has been and there always will be. Yet, I regularly meet godly Christians who recognize the need for relevance and are willing for their churches to do what needs to be done. Their problem is not willingness, it is ignorance; they don't know where to begin or what to do.

The place to begin is in your church and mine. As individual Christians and churches recognize the need and respond biblically, they will become the models and mentors for others. There can be an epidemic of revival, renewal, health, and hope.

This book is for those who want to begin. It is for those who love Christ and who love the church enough to read carefully, think clearly, and act decisively.

Leith Anderson
Wooddale Church
Eden Prairie, Minnesota

Introduction

A combination of excitement and apprehension flowed through Pastor Gary's veins. On the one hand, he felt excitement because he had recently completed seminary and was itching to get on with the business of pastoring a church. Also, he loved a challenge, and he knew Chapel Hill Community Church would be exactly that. On the other, he was a bit apprehensive. Chapel Hill had been in existence for fifteen years. During this time, its initiating pastor had grown the church to one hundred twenty people in five years. Since his departure, the church had declined to its present seventy members and had gone through five pastors with an average tenure of two years. The nagging question in the deep recesses of his mind kept asking, Would he make a difference in the life of this church? Or would he become another statistic who after two years heard the call of God to take another church or return to seminary for more studies?

Pastor Gary grew up in a non-Christian home and came to faith in Christ while in college. He was one of seventy-five million Americans called baby boomers. In his case, he was an unchurched baby boomer. He noted that his roommate, Frank, was different and spent time every morning reading his tattered Bible. Eventually, he began to ask Frank some hard questions: How do you know the Bible is true? What about the heathen who have never heard of Christ? How can Christianity be true and all other religions be false? Why would a loving God send anyone to a place called hell?

In his journey to faith, Gary occasionally accompanied Frank to a small, older traditional church located on the outskirts of the city. Perhaps this was a mistake. Gary wonders to this day if this experience was an archaic pothole on his road to faith. When he first stepped into the church, he felt as if he had been transported back

11

into the 1940s. In fact, he asked Frank if this was what life was like during the Second World War. He struggled with the music; he didn't know anyone who listened to hymns sung slowly to organ music. He questioned if these people were really serious about their faith, because many things were done poorly. The facility was in dire need of repair. The people who sang special music either forgot the words or sang them off-key. The sermons came across as boring and irrelevant and were delivered with words that he could not understand. Every time he left this church, he swore he would never go back again. Secretly, he wondered if all churches were like this one and if he would have to become like these people to be a Christian.

He did not come to faith overnight; in fact, it took about ten months. But when Gary trusted Christ, he experienced a total life change. He and Frank attended a campus Bible study, and that made the difference. The people there seemed to understand him and made a conscientious effort to answer his questions in a language he understood. The music was worshipful and upbeat, and the people were serious about their faith. After he accepted Christ, he began to spend a lot of time with some of the leaders of the group. Eventually, he committed his life to the Savior and pastoral ministry.

He never forgot his experience in that small church on the outskirts of town, however. It was indelibly stamped on his mind. He now understood what they were attempting to accomplish, but he was convinced that there must be a better way or the church in America was history. His generation would have no part of it. This conviction, like a newly planted seed, began to sprout in his soul. At seminary much of the talk among the pastoral students concerned church planting. But Gary's heart beat for the established church in spite of his experience. He loved a challenge, and he was convinced something could be done. But he had lots of questions. How does one go about accomplishing significant change in older, established churches? Is it possible? Can it be accomplished without destroying the church? Could anyone do it, or does it take a certain kind of person? And, most important, was he the right person to attempt this ministry?

Pastor Gary's situation is nothing new under the American sun. He and thousands of pastors like him want to make a difference in the numerous smaller established churches sprinkled all across

North American soil. They walk in the front doors of their new churches with big dreams and great expectations only to quietly exit the back door two or three years later with dashed dreams and wondering if somehow they had missed God's call on their lives.

Win Arn indicates that 80 to 85 percent of established American churches are either on a plateau or in decline.[1] This is a nice way of saying that 80 to 85 percent of America's churches are stagnant or dying. One article indicates that of America's 350,000 churches, 100,000 will not survive this decade.[2] Lyle Schaller writes: "An average of fifty to sixty congregations in American Protestantism choose to dissolve every week compared to perhaps five to ten that are able and willing to redefine their role."[3] In short, our established, traditional churches are in deep trouble.

At the same time, the unchurched American population is growing. A Gallup survey indicates that 44 percent of Americans were unchurched in 1988. Pete Wagner sets the figure at 55 percent in 1990, and George Barna predicts that the figure will be 65 percent by 2000. Dr. Haddon Robinson warns: "We are in an antagonist environment . . . an environment that communicates with images. We are faced with a secular society and a world that is shaped by visual images and television, a world in which God has no place. If we do not take it seriously, we are going to be left in the exhaust fumes of society."[4]

While some view this as a wrenching defeat for the church, Gallup indicates that unchurched people are interested in spiritual matters. The problem is that many of them, who are baby boomers, are not searching for truth in the typical, traditional churches. What's the solution? Picture the problem as a giant puzzle with two missing pieces that supply the answer. The first piece, and by far the best solution, is church planting. As a church planter, I predict that in the next twenty to thirty years North America will become the incubator for numerous churches all across the American landscape and ultimately the world.[5] Actually, the process has already begun. For example, four new churches currently meet on Sunday morning in one hotel located in the booming city of Plano just north of Dallas, Texas. The future of American Christianity is church planting.

The other piece of the puzzle is church revitalization. The church in North America, like Jonathan Swift's giant in *Gulliver's Travels*, has fallen asleep. The solution lies in waking the giant before it is too late.

Some raise the question, Is it too late? Can new wine be poured into old wineskins? Can established churches be revitalized? There are various answers which, if placed on a continuum, would vary from "It's impossible, don't even bother" to "Not only is it possible, we've done it!"

One extreme argues that it is too late. If the giant wakes up, he will only discover that he is hopelessly bound up in all kinds of bureaucratic red rope. Ralph Neighbour, Jr., represents this position. He writes that in 1985, after working with twenty-one pastors in an attempt to help them renew their churches, "I began to ask myself a serious question: *can new wine be put into old skins?* The answer is 'No!' Attempts at renewal don't work for one reason: our Lord told us over 2,000 years ago *it could not be done.* Every time we try to ignore His clear teaching, we fail. In retrospect, I could have saved myself 24 years of dreaming an impossible dream if I had taken His admonition literally."[6]

While not quite so dogmatic, church consultant Lyle Schaller waves a red flag and warns: "Anyone seriously interested in planned social change would be well advised to recognize two facts of life. First, despite the claims of many, relatively little is known about how to achieve predictable change. Second, much of what is known will not work."[7]

George Barna is more encouraging. In discussing the options of planting churches or revitalizing established ones, he writes:

> When I speak to groups of pastors about this information, they often ask about the difference between planting a new church and renewing an existing church using these perspectives and techniques. The fact is that it *is* substantially easier to start fresh than to recast an existing body into a new entity.
>
> There are, however, examples of churches in which a stagnant body has had new life breathed into it through a change of direction or nature.[8]

Elements of truth are found in all three positions. Both Neighbour and Schaller warn of the difficulties, discouragement, and heartache involved in church revitalization. It is not easy work. The ministry terrain is strewn with casualties. Therefore, it is imperative that Pastor Gary and those with a passion for struggling traditional churches enter the doors with open eyes. They must read the road signs before beginning their trip, especially the sign that warns, "Proceed with caution."

However, Ralph Neighbour's experience is not everyone's experience, and much has been learned about change since Schaller wrote *The Change Agent* in 1974. Barna states that birthing churches is easier than renewing churches. Actually, both have their unique problems. The question is, which set of problems do you want to live with? Any serious ministry today will present problems for pastors. Pastoring churches, whether they are new or old, is not for the lazy or faint of heart.

The answer lies not in throwing in the towel and walking away from the churches that are down for the count. Barna is correct when he indicates there are churches that have experienced new life through change. Some of these churches will push the towel aside, stand up, and get back into the fight. Notable examples are Bear Valley Baptist Church in Denver, Colorado, Wooddale Church in Eden Prairie, Minnesota, Pantego Bible Church in Arlington, Texas, and Irving Bible Church near Dallas, Texas. These ministries and countless others indicate that it is possible to pour new wine into old wineskins. This means that it is possible to take advantage of the resources of the typical established North American church such as its existing people, property, and facilities, which otherwise might be squandered or lost.

This book will assist leaders like Pastor Gary as they initiate and work through the revitalization process. It is designed to be a companion as they navigate their ministries through the ocean of change. In light of the needs of so many churches, its pages should quickly become frayed and soiled. It is organized into four parts.

Part 1 describes the problem of change, demonstrates the urgent need for renewal, and provides a backdrop for the next three parts. It consists of two chapters. The first calls attention to the tidal wave of change sweeping across America in the decade of the 1990s. The second shows the impact of this wave on the traditional, established church and how it has resulted in an acceleration of the number of unchurched persons in America.

Part 2 presents the personnel for change. Most leaders interested in transition ministries are asking the "how" question. They believe the answer to their problems lies in discovering the process of change. They want to know *how* to accomplish significant, planned change in their ministries. The process is important, but recent studies indicate that *who* is as important as *how*. Part 2 will answer the question, What kinds of people are revitalization pastors? It contains two chapters that explore the divine-design concept and paint a portrait of what a revitalization leader looks like.

Part 3 will probe the "how" question. Once the portrait is on the leadership canvas, the next issue is the practice of revitalization. Part 3 consists of five chapters, which escort change agents through five steps of revitalization. The first chapter alerts the change agent to some major reasons why people do not like to change. The second presents the people of change. It divides the ministry constituency into four groups according to their response to change. The third focuses on the times for change and identifies the various "windows of opportunity" that open and close in the life of a ministry. The fourth covers the process of change, which consists of three stages that characterize change in any church regardless of its size or location. The last chapter presents several change principles that are helpful tools to pastors as they lead their churches through the three-stage process. The application of these tools to the process results in a tailor-made program designed for each pastor's unique ministry.

Part 4 displays the product of change. It answers the question, What does a renewed church look like? This chapter provides a snapshot of a revitalized church consisting of seven key biblical principles that give direction for the church. They are a Great Commission vision; a strong, servant leadership; a well-mobilized lay army; a culturally relevant ministry; an authentic, holistic worship; a relevant, biblical evangelism; and a robust network of small groups.

How might you use the material in this book most effectively? First, change agents should read through each chapter individually. At the end of the book are worksheets designed to help make personal-life or ministry applications. Once you have digested the material and are ready to move in a new direction, provide your board or the appropriate people with copies of this book and work through the material with them. The use of an outside source such as a consultant, or in this case a book, adds to your credibility.

Part 1
The Problem of Change

Leading Churches
to See
the Need for Change

1

Megachange and America
Living for Change

I have ridden on a roller coaster one time. It was both exciting and frightening to weave back and forth, up and down on a small track at breakneck speed while catching an occasional glimpse of the ground thirty to fifty feet below. I was glad to get off when the ride ended; I swore I would never do it again.

America is exploding with change as much as at any given time in the history of the nation. We live in a decade of megachange, when everything changes at breakneck speed and many people are living for change.[1] In the last twenty to thirty years, Western society in general and America in particular has climbed on board the roller coaster of change only to discover that it cannot get off. And there seems to be no end to the ride in sight.

The result is accelerating, turbulent times. The basic way we did things yesterday is no longer the way we do them today. What was appropriate for the 1940s and 1950s is not appropriate for the 1990s. That which was but a figment of the imagination in the 1950s is reality today. But how much change has taken place, and what has actually changed? More important, what impact has change had on our lives, and what can we do about it? Is there a way to anticipate such change?

Statistics and Adjectives of Change

Various writers of different backgrounds have dared to put some figures on the accelerating change in America. From the business perspective, Michael Gerber in *The E-Myth* writes of change in general: "Today's world is a difficult place. Mankind has experienced more change in the past twenty years than in the 2,000 that preceded them."[2]

Faith Popcorn is the name adopted by a female trends analyst. In an article published in *The Dallas Morning News* in 1991, she is quoted as "predicting a 'socioquake'—a grass-roots shake-up of society prompted by more changes in the next 10 years than in the last 90."[3]

George Barna is a Christian and the founder and president of Barna Research Group, a full-service marketing research company in Glendale, California. In *The Frog in the Kettle* he alerts us to the acceleration of change over the next years in terms of the amount of information that will soon be at the fingertips of the average person. He writes, "We now have only 3 percent of the information that will be available to us by 2010."[4] Consequently, the next few years will see an explosion of information.

I have used the term *megachange* to make the point that America is experiencing change in a way unprecedented in its history. Others use similar adjectives and words to make the same point. Michael Gerber speaks of "accelerated change" and the "insatiable vortex of change."[5] Robert Tucker describes change as "oncoming, overwhelming, accelerating."[6] Joel Arthur Barker writes of "dramatic" and "extraordinary" change.[7] Tom Peters describes the impact of change: "The world has not just 'turned upside down.' It is turning in every which way at an accelerating pace."[8]

Kinds of Change

The changes of the past twenty years have been broad and diverse. While most noticeable in the social, economic, political, and technological arenas, change has left no rock unturned. It has touched every area of life. In *Discovering the Future*, futurist Joel Arthur Barker provides a quite complete but abbreviated compendium of some of the fundamental changes which have taken place in the world in the last twenty years.

> The introduction of environmentalism (everything living is interconnected; there is no such thing as a free lunch) as a legitimate way of perceiving the world.
> Terrorism as an everyday activity.

20

Rampant inflation in the United States during the 1970s and 1980s.

Deregulation of banking, the airlines, the telecommunications, and trucking industries.

The loss of the United States' position as the leading edge manufacturer of the world (for example, of VCRs). (All of a sudden we find United States' products not the "premium.")

VCRs.

Civil rights.

The growth of participatory management in the United States.

The loss of respect for major institutions such as the Supreme Court, the police, the federal government, the Congress.

The almost total disappearance of union power.

The emergence of information as a key resource.

Public language on TV and radio incorporating cursing and strong sexual connotation within normal programming.

Cohabitation as an acceptable substitute for marriage.

The collapse of nuclear power as a viable energy option for the United States.

A new appreciation of "small is beautiful" and the rejection of "big is always better."

The common use of satellite communications.

The disappearance of the idea that continuous growth is automatically good.

The vast amount of data exchanged via computers worldwide.

The "uncloseting" of gays and other previously hidden minorities.

Fiber optics.

The new importance of the role of women in business and politics.

Energy conservation as a new attitude in the United States.

The women's movement.

The growing necessity of cable TV.

The number of people getting regular aerobic exercise every day.

Breaking up of AT&T and the formation of the Baby Bells.

Japan as a producer of the highest quality products.

Cellular phones.

The collapse of the savings and loan industry.

Faxing.

Yogurt "ice cream."

Rap music.

Superconductivity at warmer temperatures.

ʾouse Effect.

...ᴜer of people eating a healthy diet by choice.

ᴦhe explosion of the use of personal computers in the home and office.

Biotechnology.

Republicans saying a large deficit is okay.[9]

Impact of Change

The statistics and adjectives of change are indicative of the profound impact change is having on all areas of American life. In times of exploding change, a business-as-usual mentality is out of the question. Gerber writes:

> Boundaries that once served us—geographically, politically, socially, emotionally—no longer exist. The rules are constantly changing. But people cannot live without boundaries, without structure, without rules. So new ones have sprung up and proliferated in order to fill the void left by those that no longer seem to serve our "new age" condition.
>
> Unfortunately, in a world of accelerated change there is little time for rules to take hold. As soon as the new rules are upon us, they too are swallowed up in the insatiable vortex of change, followed all too quickly by more rules, and then still more.[10]

Along the same lines, Barker writes:

> In the last twenty years, all of Western society has been through extraordinary turbulent times. We have been living in a time when fundamental rules, the basic ways we do things, have been altered dramatically. . . . These kinds of dramatic changes are extremely important because they have created in us a special sense of impermanence which generates tremendous discomfort.[11]

Robert Tucker focuses on the impact of change in the corporate world. He writes:

> As I travel the corporate speaking circuit, consulting and meeting with business leaders in a wide variety of industries, I hear a common refrain: The pace of change has exploded. In industry after industry I learn of companies that have been severely crippled or

destroyed because of an inadequate or inappropriate response to rapid change: the Beverly Hills real estate syndicator that did not respond to changes in the tax laws; the office products dealers in Boston forced to close because of competition from a new office supplies superstore; the Minneapolis resort that nearly had to cancel its summer season for lack of employees.[12]

Anticipating Change

All of this change appears ominous to any organization, whether sacred or secular, and raises a pragmatic question: Is there a way to anticipate coming change? Certainly, the ability to successfully lead organizations such as churches through change is enhanced by the ability to anticipate change. But is this possible? Does God still raise up prophets who foresee the future with great vision and clarity as in the days of the Old Testament?

The key to anticipating the future lies in understanding fads, trends, megatrends, and paradigms. Each relates to change but differs in terms of time and intensity. Fads reflect changes that last for the shortest period of time and have the least influence or impact. They may last only a few days or a few years. Once they are gone, they are soon forgotten. Some examples would be in children's toys, adults' games, haircuts, clothing styles, and so on.

Trends last longer and have greater impact than fads. In the book *Megatrends 2000*, John Naisbitt seems to use the term *megatrends* synonymously with trends or the "most important trends."[13] He writes: "Megatrends do not come and go easily. These large social, economic, political, and technological changes are slow to form, and once in place, they influence us for some time—between seven and ten years, or longer. They have the scope and feel of a decade's worth of change."[14] In *Megatrends 2000*, Naisbitt identifies new trends for the 1990s: a global economic boom, a renaissance in the arts, the emergence of free-market socialism, the privatization of the welfare state, the rise of the Pacific Rim as the new world-trade center, the emergence of women in leadership, an age of biotechnology, a religious revival of the third millennium, and the empowerment of the individual.

Paradigms have the greatest impact in terms of change. Joel Arthur Barker writes: "A paradigm is a set of rules and regulations that: 1) defines boundaries; and 2) tells you what to do to be successful within those boundaries. (Success is measured by the problems you solve using these rules and regulations.)"[15] There are many paradigms in this world, and each tells us that there is a game and how to participate in that game successfully. For example, there is a paradigm for marathons in America. While the American runner may participate in shorter marathons, the longest marathon is twenty-six miles. Athletes who participate in the Boston Marathon understand that it is twenty-six miles. To ask runners to go any further is to push them beyond the point of human endurance. A technological example is the Swiss watch manufacturers' paradigm for watches prior to the 1970s. They built watches with gears, springs, and jeweled bearings. Also, they ticked. Some other object might look like a watch and even keep time, but if it did not meet these specifications, as far as the Swiss were concerned, it was not a watch.

When a paradigm shifts, the result is a new game with a new set of rules. For example, I predict that the American paradigm for the twenty-six-mile marathon will change in the future. Presently, Americans think that twenty-six miles is the maximum of human endurance. How could anyone run further? Yet, the Tarahumara Indians, a tribe living in Northern Mexico, run the equivalent of seventy-mile marathons. The difference is they do this almost every day. They have no automobiles and run everywhere they go. It is only a matter of time before American runners discover this and begin to run seventy-mile marathons.

Another example is the Swiss watch paradigm. The Swiss, themselves, invented the new paradigm quartz watch. But it was electronic. It had no gears, springs, or jeweled bearings. As far as they were concerned, it was not a watch. The market would be slow to accept it. So they refused to adjust and by the 1980s their market share plummeted to below 10 percent. The quartz watch revolution has practically destroyed the Swiss domination of the market. Barker argues that a number of these shifts have and are taking place that have caused much of the turbulence of the last twenty years.

To understand this turbulent, whirling vortex of change, you must realize that behind the various trends and megatrends there has been a shift in paradigms. Barker calls attention to Naisbitt's megatrends and writes that "if you trace back to the beginning of those trends, you will find a paradigm shift."[16] Basically, a paradigm shifts and the result is a new trend or megatrend.

24

Consequently, the key to anticipating the future is to look for paradigm shifts that are currently taking place that will produce the trends and megatrends of the future. Barker offers some help. First, he argues that there are certain conditions that trigger paradigm shifts. The primary condition is that the present paradigm ceases to solve all the problems. A problem surfaces and the paradigm offers no present solution. Over a period of time, more problems begin to build up. The current paradigm continues to solve problems, but a current mass of unsolved problems is accumulating below the surface. Eventually, they trigger a major change, which results in a new paradigm. Consequently, for leaders to anticipate significant change, they must look for and keep track of accumulating, unresolved problems.

An example is the present decline in attendance in the more traditional, established churches across America. While this will be explored more fully in the next chapter, the church paradigm of the 1940s and 1950s is producing all kinds of problems for churches in the 1990s. The primary manifestation is that these churches are not reaching the baby boom and baby bust generations, with the result that they are rapidly dwindling in size. Some argue that the old paradigm still works and all that is needed to solve the problems is to work harder. Increasingly, others are calling for and implementing a new paradigm to reach the generation of the 1990s and future generations for Christ.

Next, Barker asks: What kind of person is a paradigm shifter? The answer is simple: an outsider. The reason people are able to come into a situation and develop new paradigms to solve the problems of the current paradigm is because they are not immersed in that paradigm. They look at things in fresh, innovative ways. They are catalysts of change who are willing to take risks and develop a whole new set of rules for solving old problems. A struggling, declining church in the Dallas-Fort Worth metroplex replaced its former pastor with a twenty-nine-year-old man with a background in business, leadership development, and parachurch ministry. He was an outsider who brought a fresh perspective to an old paradigm. Today this revitalized church is experiencing a new outreach into its community.

Finally, Barker focuses on the results of a paradigm shift. He calls this the paradigm effect.[17] Those who adopt the new paradigm see things in ways they had never seen before. They become empowered by the new set of rules to perceive new answers to old, unsolved problems. Thus, the paradigm acts as a filter or pair of glasses through which the world is viewed differently. Those who reject the new paradigm continue to see the world through a different set of lenses. They are blind as far as the new paradigm is concerned. The problem is not that they are unintelligent but that their old paradigm does not allow them to perceive what is actually taking place in the world.

America is exploding with change, and behind all these changes are various new paradigms. I will return to the issue of paradigms in later chapters. However, a critical question for the American church is: How has exploding change affected it? The answer is in the next chapter.

2

Megachange and the Church
Dying for Change

Pastor Gary knew well the fifteen-year history of Chapel Hill Community Church. A careful scholar, he had done his homework with painstaking accuracy. The first five years were characterized by pulsating growth. However, at the end of those years some major problems erupted, and the church landed on a substantial plateau. Eventually, the founding pastor heard God's call to move to another church and was gone within a few weeks. Soon after, the church began a ten-year decline that has resulted in its current membership of seventy people.

Pastor Gary could not comprehend a ministry of maintenance to seventy people. Maintenance was not his style. He was by no stretch of the imagination a church custodian. If Chapel Hill extended a call, and he accepted, he knew the situation would have to improve or he would languish.

This would require significant change and lots of it. The pastor who would make a difference in this church must be a skilled agent of intentional change. He understood all this and that the entire venture was a major risk. But he loved a challenge. He also had questions, lots of them. One in particular bothered him: Was Chapel Hill an exception to the norm, or was its life cycle typical of other churches in America?

At the end of this century and the dawning of a new era, the evidence is clear that the American church, like Chapel Hill Community Church, is not doing well. As Leith Anderson indicates, it is dying for change.[1] The typical church in the fast-paced 1990s has checked into the hospital and spends much of its time heavily sedated and sleeping under the covers of the 1940s and 1950s. But exactly what has gone wrong? What is the diagnosis? The problem is threefold: The church is in a general decline, and many churches expire while the nonchurched population of America grows. This has created a spiritual void, which is being partially filled by a number of cults and nonreligious groups.

The Decline of the American Church

Kirk Hadaway, a church-growth research specialist with the Southern Baptist Convention, writes: "The typical church in almost any American denomination is either on a plateau or declining in membership and participation. Rapid growth is atypical, and among older congregations the pattern is even more pronounced—plateau and decline are the rule; growth is the rare exception."[2]

In *The Pastor's Manual for Effective Ministry*, Win Arn explains: "In the years following World War II thousands of new churches were established. Today, of the approximately 350,000 churches in America, four out of five are either plateaued or declining."[3] He explains further: "In the normal life cycle of churches, there is birth, and in time, death. Many churches begin to plateau and/or show decline around their 15th–18th year."[4] Then he sums up the current status of the church in America with the following statistic: "80–85 percent of the churches in America are on the downside of this growth cycle."[5] Does this exceptionally high figure accurately represent the state of the American church? Studies of both mainline and conservative churches indicate that it does.

Mainline Churches

Roof and McKinney define mainline churches as "the dominant, culturally established faiths held by the majority of Americans."[6] Mainline churches are also characterized by their liberal theology.

Figure 1 represents a study of church membership for five mainline denominations based on the *Yearbook of American and Canadian Churches, 1988*. This study compares figures reported in 1965 with those in 1988 in the Christian Church (Disciples of Christ), Episcopal Church, the Presbyterian Church (U.S.A.), the United Methodist Church, and the United Church of Christ.[7] In all cases, these denominations show significant decline. Commenting on them and others, Roof and McKinney write:

28

For all these churches, those losses represented an abrupt and dramatic turnaround in their privileged status and respectability: churches seemingly as American as apple pie and the Fourth of July suddenly fell upon hard times. As many as 10 of the largest Protestant denominations were in the throes of what can only be described as a serious religious depression.[8]

Figure 1
Mainline Churches

	1965	1988
Christian Church (Disciples of Christ)	2 million	1 million
Episcopal Church	3.4 million	2.5 million
Presbyterian Church (U.S.A.)	4.3 million	2.9 million
United Methodist Church	11 million	9 million
United Church of Christ	2 million	1.6 million

Conservative Churches

How are the conservative churches doing? These churches are represented by those who are evangelical in their beliefs such as the fundamentalists, the charismatics, and the Pentecostals (some would include the Catholic and Mormon churches). Figure 2 is a study of the church membership statistics from 1965 to 1988 for the Assemblies of God, the Christian and Missionary Alliance, the Lutheran Church—Missouri Synod, and the Southern Baptists.[9] All of these churches except the Lutheran Church—Missouri Synod show strong growth.

America's largest Protestant denomination, the Southern Baptist Convention—despite several years of internal conflict—appears to have experienced a steady, significant growth pattern from ten million in 1965 to almost fifteen million in 1988. Upon further examination, however, internal evidence indicates a plateau or possible

Figure 2
Conservative Churches

	1965	1988
Assemblies of God	572,000	2,100,000
Christian and Missionary Alliance	64,000	259,000
Lutheran Church—Missouri Synod	2,692,000	2,604,000
Southern Baptist Convention	10,770,000	14,812,000

decline in recent years. An article in the Southern Baptist publication, *Missions USA*, reported the following:

> The Southern Baptist stall in 1987 is not a cause for alarm, but "it should be fully discussed and explored," pollster George Gallup claimed. In the church year, ending September 30, 1987, some denominational programs reported small changes and had gains or totals smaller than have been seen in decades, according to statistics compiled by the Baptist Sunday School Board's research department. "Southern Baptist statistics appear to represent a leveling out rather than a reversal or sudden turnaround," Gallup said when asked to evaluate the denomination's most recent statistical results. Compared with other mainline denominations in the United States, Southern Baptists have defied national trends for years. The modest downward reports in the denomination's key program areas represent a flattening out of what had been moving up for years.[10]

Helen Parmley provides an explanation for this apparent contradiction in *The Dallas Morning News*. She wisely cautions that those who use the *Yearbook of American and Canadian Churches* must consider how it collects its statistics. She writes:

> The yearbook, which probably has the most accurate statistics of American churches, is widely used and quoted. But before taking the figures to the bank, consider some of the methods denominations use to compile those statistics. According to the statistics in the yearbook, membership in the Southern Baptist Convention rose in 1989 from 14.8 million to 14.9 million, and membership in the Presbyterian Church (U.S.A.) fell from 2.9 million to 2.8 million. The Southern Baptists, however, record two membership lists. One is a "resident" membership, the other is a "total" membership. For example, in 1989, First Baptist Church of Dallas—the largest congregation in the denomination—recorded 13,271 "resident" members and 28,000 "total" members. The church's sanctuary seats about 2,500 people and has three Sunday morning services. The Presbyterian denomination, on the other hand, encourages its churches to keep membership rolls "clean" by assessing an annual per-capita tax. In 1989, for instance, the denominational tax per member was $3.70. Some denominations accept baptized newborns as members, but other denominations don't. They wait until they are old enough to give testimony or be confirmed. Although the National Baptist Convention, U.S.A., Inc., is listed in the yearbook as the nation's fourth largest Protestant denomina-

tion, its latest membership count of 5.5 million was taken in 1958.[11]

The Assemblies of God—the largest Pentecostal group in America—quadrupled in size from 1965 to 1988. The Christian and Missionary Alliance has quadrupled over the same period of time. Peter Wagner attributes much of this growth to strong church planting programs within the two groups. The Assemblies of God intend to establish five thousand new churches in the 1990s, and the Christian and Missionary Alliance leadership has announced "1,000 more by 1994!"[12] Also, Lyle Schaller confirms that the key to growth is church planting. He writes, "It continues to be the most useful and productive component of any denominational church growth strategy."[13]

However, in light of Parmley's information above, we must be careful to probe these statistics and those of other growing churches with key questions. First, we must ask if these figures represent "resident" or "total" membership. While the Southern Baptists' total membership showed significant increase, the resident membership reflected a plateau or possible decline.

Another key question is, What kind of growth are these churches experiencing? Churches grow in one or a combination of three ways. The first is transfer growth, which is the movement of people from one similar church to another. The second is biological growth. Members have babies who grow up and eventually join the church. The third is conversion growth, which focuses on winning lost people to Christ. Carroll, Johnson, and Marty observe that in the 1960s and 1970s some conservative-church growth also involved "switchers"—proselytes from different denominations.

> Thus it seems that conservative church growth, at least in the groups studied, comes primarily through a kind of circulation process, by which evangelicals move from one conservative church to another. To a lesser extent, new additions are the offspring of members reared in an evangelical culture. Proselyte-type converts are typically "switchers" from other nonevangelical or conservative denominations; however, this is the least important source of new members. Bibby and Brinkerhoff conclude that conservative churches do a better job of retaining those already familiar with

31

evangelical culture—both transfers and children of members—than moderate and liberal churches do in retaining their members.[14]

While the Southern Baptists, the Assemblies of God, and the Christian and Missionary Alliance churches report growth due to either an emphasis on church planting and/or transfer growth, many evangelical churches that are not faring well do not appear in the yearbook. In fact, most evangelical churches' populations are in decline.[15] One example is the churches that loosely make up the Bible-church movement. Many of these churches are pastored by the graduates of nondenominational Bible colleges and seminaries known primarily for their pulpit exposition of the Scriptures. As I travel and spend time in these churches I find evidence that the majority are plateaued or in decline.

The Death of American Churches

Not only are United States churches plateaued and declining, many are dying. In past decades, churches might decline to twenty or thirty people and linger at that size with flat vital signs. Their life support was infusions of money supplied by individuals or a denomination outside the church.

All that has changed as the twentieth century draws to a close. Lyle Schaller writes, "An average of fifty to sixty congregations in American Protestantism choose to dissolve every week compared to perhaps five to ten that are able and willing to redefine their role."[16] Win Arn indicates that 3500 to 4000 churches die every year.[17] An article in *Ministry* states: "America is running out of churches. It's true. Studies show that, in the next few years, 100,000 churches will close their doors—an extraordinary figure when you realize there are only 350,000 churches existing in our country."[18] *Christianity Today* reports, "Many church observers believe most of the generation of churches planted just after World War II is in the final stages of institutional life."[19]

Why are all these churches expiring? *Christianity Today* offers several explanations. One that affects independent churches is the lack of outside financial and structural support from a denomination. Another is the failure of the church in high-density urban areas to meet a wide variety of choices and demands. A third is the inability of 70 percent of the churches in America to break through the "200 barrier," which is the size necessary in a metropolitan setting to provide the services people expect from the church in the 1990s. A fourth is the lack of vision on the part of those in the pulpit, and the negative impact on people in the pew—they have no sense of direction. A fifth is a decline in evangelism, accompanied by decreases in attendance and financial strength. In fact, the two most common symptoms of church death are decrease in attendance and in finances.[20] The future is clear. At least a third or more of America's established, stereotypical churches will not survive this decade.

Some conservative churches are experiencing growth, but it is not as significant as the yearbook figures might indicate. Outside of church planting efforts, much of this growth is recirculation of the saints. The mainline churches are in a significant decline, and the future looks dim. At the same time, a large number of churches are dying. Consequently, Win Arn's estimate that 80 to 85 percent of the churches in the United States (both mainline and conservative) are plateaued or in decline proves accurate.

The Growth of the Unchurched

While the American church is struggling, the unchurched population is growing. This raises three questions.

Who Are the Unchurched?

The American unchurched population consists primarily of baby boomers and baby busters. *The baby boom* is the term for the explosion of births which took place between 1946 and 1964. The boomers, who are entering midlife in the 1990s, make up more than one-third the American population and are in excess of 76 million people. Early in 1990, every other household was headed by one, and in the 1990s they will have a potential discretionary income of $18 billion. They are a highly educated generation; one-quarter of them have college degrees.

The baby-bust generation are the children of the baby boomers. They believe they have inherited from their parents a world that will make it harder for them to get ahead in life. They are also highly pessimistic about the long-term fate of their generation. Currently, America is passing through a baby boomlet. McIntosh writes:

In 1989 births hit 4 million, the largest number of births since the post World War II baby boom ended in 1964. Labeled baby busters due to the fact that they are a "bust" generation in comparison to that of their parents, this new generation is now between the ages of 8 and 25 years old.[21]

McIntosh divides the busters into three broad groups: "There are the older busters 20–25 years old, teenage busters 13–19 years old, and younger busters 8–12 years old."[22]

Since they are the children of baby boomers, the baby busters have become the second generation unchurched. The difference, however, is that whereas the boomers dropped out of church, the busters were not in church to begin with. They are what George Hunter calls "ignostics." He writes: "The most important consequence of secularization is the growing Western populations who have no Christian background, memory, vocabulary, or assumptions; they are 'ignostics,' who do not know what Christians are talking about."[23]

The situation appears to be worsening. An article in *The Dallas Morning News* subtitled, "Parents returning to religion to give children moral training," reports the following incident:

> John and Susan Jackson realized their firstborn son's spiritual development was lacking when he confused church with Church's. Blake, then 4, had slept overnight at his grandparents'. The next morning, the grandparents prepared for worship services. Mrs. Jackson said her son asked to stay longer, saying his grandparents were "going to Church's, and I want to stay for fried chicken."[24]

John and Susan Jackson were church dropouts from the baby-boom generation or first generation of nonchurched. Their son Blake, second generation nonchurched, had little awareness of the church. When his grandparents mentioned going to church, he did not picture the ornate building on the corner with a steeple and a cross. Instead, he thought of a chain of fast-food chicken stores called Church's Fried Chicken.

How Many Are Unchurched?

In 1978 George Gallup surveyed American adults age eighteen or older and discovered that 41 percent were unchurched.[25] He defined the unchurched as "those who are not members of a church or have not attended services in the previous six months other than for special religious holidays, weddings, funerals or the like."[26] In 1988 he again conducted the poll. It was based on personal interviews with 2556 adults eighteen or older in more than 300 scientifically selected localities across the nation. This time the figure had climbed to 44 percent.[27] He adds, "The percentage of unchurched adults, based on the Bureau of Labor Statistics population estimate, projected to 61 million in 1978 and 78 million in 1988."[28]

The evidence indicates that in the 1990s the figure continues to move upward. Peter Wagner writes that at the beginning of the 1990s the number of unchurched people exceeds Gallup's figure. He estimates the number of churched people to be around 45 percent. Thus the number of unchurched is 55 percent.[29] In *How to Reach Secular People*, Hunter estimates the United States' constant church attendance at 40 percent.[30] So the unchurched would be 60 percent. The *Leadership Journal* confirms this same figure.[31] George Barna predicts that by the year 2000, "church attendance on Sunday mornings will decrease to about 35 percent of the population on any given weekend."[32] This means the number of unchurched would climb to 65 percent by the end of the decade. As I travel around the country, many pastors tell me that the figure in their communities is much higher than this. They would place the number somewhere in the range of 75 to 90 percent, even in the South. Randy Frasee, who pastors Pantego Bible Church in Arlington, Texas, which is part of the Bible Belt, estimates that 75 to 80 percent of Arlington is unchurched. He states, "The Bible Belt has lost a few of its notches."

Can They Be Reached?

Indications are that the unchurched could be reached in this generation. The fact that they are not in church does not mean they are uninterested in spiritual matters. In fact, Gallup's study revealed a strong potential for them to return to church. He writes, "But while the number of 'belongers' has declined over the past decade, the number of 'believers' has actually increased." Then he concludes, "The new survey indicates that there is considerable potential for a return of the 'unchurched' to more active church life."[33] This is because they are more religious than a decade ago; they hold high levels of religious belief; a large proportion provide

35

religious training for their children; 58 percent are considering a return to church; and so on.

What is important about the baby-bust generation is that they are at a young age where people are reached more easily with the gospel of Christ. Barna writes: "Research consistently shows that people are most likely to accept Christ as their Savior before they reach the age of 18. Currently, about two-thirds of all decisions for Christ happen by that age."[34]

The problem is not a lack of interest in spiritual matters, it is a lack of interest in the established, old-paradigm church. Jack Sims writes that the typical boomer attends church only 6.2 times per year.[35] He explains why in the following:

> Most of the baby boomers I have interviewed describe their experience with church and religious media as boring, irrelevant or high-pressured. They say things like: "I don't like the music. It sounds old-fashioned and strange." "It's too one-sided politically." "They are always asking for money." Some young believers I meet as I travel around the country are trying to hang on to religion programmed to the taste of the older generation. Others are hoping to find spiritual homes within parachurch organizations. But a growing number are deciding that the cultural pain of living inside the traditional organizations is greater than the pain of pulling up their spiritual and emotional roots. Tom Stipe, the 33-year-old pastor of Colorado's second largest church says, "The church is the last standing barrier between our generation and Jesus."[36]

George Barna writes, "From 1987 to 1991, boomers returned to the church in a major way."[37] He explains, "Millions of boomers were driven by a desire to raise their youngsters with some formal religious education. Toward the end, they temporarily suspended their own concerns about churches and came back to the fold primarily for the sake of their offspring."[38] Barna concludes: "Being rational people, though, boomers also constantly analyze their environment and compare the benefits received against the costs incurred. After a few years of gathering information necessary to draw a conclusion, the verdict is now in. The church is guilty of irrelevance. Kids or no kids, literally hundreds of thousands of boomers are exiting."[39]

Benton Johnson, a sociology professor at the University of Oregon, Dean Hoge, a Presbyterian layman and sociology professor at Catholic University, and Donald Luidens, an associate professor of sociology at Hope College in Holland, Michigan, conducted a study financed by the Lilly endowment which revealed, "The 'lost generation' of baby boomers who left mainline Protestantism in the 1970s and '80s is not coming back, and their churches will exert even less of a hold on their children."[40] However, in the same article John Mulder, president of Louisville Presbyterian Theological Seminary, encourages churches not to write off baby boomers, because they are still seeking some way to make sense of evil, suffering, and injustice. He says, "It may be that the jury is still out on whether they return to church . . . when children come along and when they face life crises with the onset of middle age."[41] Benton Johnson adds, "It's just that the church doesn't do anything for them."[42]

The Growth of Cults and Nonevangelicals

The fact that the American church struggles and the unchurched population grows is frightening enough. But in addition, this has created a spiritual vacuum which a number of growing cults and nonevangelical groups are quickly filling.

One is the Mormons. Recently, *U.S. News & World Report* stated:

> Today the Church of Jesus Christ of Latter Day Saints, better known as the Mormon Church, is one of the world's richest and fastest-growing religious movements. Since World War II, its ranks have quadrupled to more than 8.3 million members worldwide. With 4.5 million U.S. members, Mormons already outnumber Presbyterians and Episcopalians combined. If current trends hold, by some estimates they will number 250 million worldwide by 2080 and surpass all but the Roman Catholic Church among Christian bodies.[43]

According to the *Yearbook of American and Canadian Churches*, the Church of Jesus Christ of Latter Day Saints doubled as it grew from 1,789,175 in 1965 to 3,860,000 in 1985 (figure 3).[44] In *Megatrends 2000*, John Naisbitt writes, "Mormons celebrated the 'best' year in their 158-year history in 1987, when they joined a record 274,000 new adherents."[45]

What are the reasons for this astounding growth? *U.S. News & World Report* indicates several. First is the church's unique doctrines and strong emphasis on family and wholesome living that attracts many who are disillusioned with traditional Christianity. Second is

37

Figure 3
Church of Jesus Christ of Latter Day Saints

1965	1970	1975	1980	1985
1,789,175	2,073,146	2,336,715	2,811,000	3,860,000

their aggressive worldwide missionary effort that involves more than 60 percent of all Mormons between the ages of 18 and 22 in preaching the Mormon Gospel door to door. Third is the strong support that church members give in their time and money. However, what ultimately attracts new converts is their distinctive tenets. For example, the church believes that only "sons of perdition"—former believers who betray the church—will experience eternal punishment. All others will experience some aspect of the "telestial kingdom." Also, church members baptize their dead nonbeliever relatives by undergoing proxy baptism in their place.[46]

Another is the Jehovah's Witnesses. The yearbook reports that they, like the Mormons, have doubled in the last twenty years— growing from 330,358 in 1965 to 804,639 in 1990 (figure 4).[47] I suspect that a primary reason for their growth is their aggressive worldwide missionary effort.

A third is the New Age movement. Naisbitt estimates that the unorganized New Agers represent 5 to 10 percent of the American population.[48] Regarding their future in America along with other groups, Barna writes:

> Groups outside evangelical and mainline Christianity will continue to expand rapidly. The Mormon church will reach 10 million members by 2000, largely due to their emphasis on relationships between members. Eastern faiths, especially Buddhism and Islam, will more than double in the number of adherents. The New Age religions will prosper, although many of the groups that will be prolific by 2000 are not yet in existence.[49]

Figure 4
Jehovah's Witnesses

1965	1970	1975	1980	1985	1990
330,358	388,920	560,897	565,309	730,441	804,639

38

However, the growth of the cults and the evidence of interest in spiritual matters indicate that the decade of the 1990s and the early twenty-first century could be a time of unprecedented opportunity for reaching the unchurched for the Savior. The critical question is: What is the typical, established American church willing to do to reach lost people? The Father was willing to give up his Son (John 3:16). The Son was willing to give up his life (Rom. 5:8). Paul was willing to give up his salvation (Rom. 9:3). What is the church willing to give up to reach this vast, unchurched generation? Would it be willing to change its style of Christian music, to stop asking repeatedly for money, and to program itself to the tastes of the younger generation, as well as of the older generation?

Part 2
The Personnel for Change

Finding the Right Leaders
for Change

3

The Preparation for Assessment
Understanding How You Are Wired

Pastor Gary was surprised and amazed. The situation at Chapel Hill Community Church mirrored the typical American church described in chapter 2. He realized that this church was not unique and that numerous other pastors attempt to minister daily in similar circumstances. But while many of his seminary friends had washed their hands of the established, typical church and opted for church planting, he felt even more intensely the challenge to enter a ministry of change and church renewal.

A question lurked deep within Pastor Gary's soul. It haunted him whenever he thought about Chapel Hill Community Church, which lately was much of the time, for the church had invited him to be their pastor. On occasion, he would wake up in the middle of the night, sit up in bed, and ask, Am I the kind of man who can lead a church through change, or will I fail in the process? Would I destroy it, or could it destroy me? At the very beginning, he was able to ignore these questions. Now he would have to face them head-on because the answer to them would be his answer to the church.

It is imperative that anyone going into ministry ask a number of questions at the onset. The critical question that few ever ask when called to an older, traditional church is, Am I a change agent? The answer lies in the assessment process. Since the area of assessment is so new to those pursuing professional ministry, this chapter will orient prospective pastors in general and change agents in particular to self-assessment. The next chapter will answer the question,

Who can lead churches through the change process? The focus of this brief orientation is on the purpose and value of assessment.[1]

The Value of Assessment

Pastor Gary's question underlies the value of a good assessment program. It also mirrors the predicament of thousands of thinking young leaders across the country who have already prepared for or are contemplating Christian ministry. A good assessment process proves valuable in two ways. The first is of personal value and the second organizational value.

Personal Value

How might a self-assessment personally benefit those pursuing Christian ministry? Three benefits could make the difference between a lifetime of ministry fulfillment or a short-term ministry disaster.

KNOWING WHO YOU ARE

The first benefit of a well-designed assessment program is knowing who you are. For many this can be a frightening notion. Their hearts begin to palpitate and their hands perspire. What is an explanation for this stressful response? In the past, most assessment has been pathological. Job applicants or students enrolling in school have taken pathological tools designed to expose any trace of psychological abnormality or dysfunctional behavior. The applicant suspects this and takes an instrument such as the MMPI (*The Minnesota Multiphasic Personality Inventory*) with some fear and anxiety.

The purpose of the pathological approach is to determine what is wrong with a person. The advantage to this approach for leaders in Christian ministry is that it helps them discover and know more about their depravity. But the emphasis has been one-sided and is in need of balance. Another dimension to the process is more positive. It involves probing a person's dignity and discovering the positive side as well as the negative. Its purpose is to determine what is right.

This dimension looks at Christian leaders as image bearers who reflect in numerous ways the unique stamp of divine creation (Gen. 1:26; James 3:9). One of the arguments over the centuries for the existence of God is universal cosmic design. Simply stated, it argues that behind every design is a designer. There is no question

44

that our world reflects a masterful cosmic design, and God is the master designer who is responsible for it all (Ps. 19:1). Assessment of Christian leaders attempts to help them detect and understand their unique designs as a part of a universe of intentional creative design.

Secularists recognize the presence of design in the lives of people. However, they would argue that people are born into this world much as a blank slate or an unwritten book. Then the individual's environment, consisting of parents, peers, and teachers, writes on the slate or in the book, which ultimately determines the individual's personality. The other side of this explanation is personal accountability. If a person becomes a criminal or a misfit, then society, not the individual, is ultimately at fault.

Other secularists argue that a man is godlike and has the ability to be and do whatever he desires in this world. One presidential candidate expressed this view when he said that he dreamed of an America where every child could grow up to be whatever he or she wanted to be.

While both a person's environment and human will can and often do have a powerful effect on that life, the biblical concept of divine design provides a balanced perspective. It recognizes some influence of society and the will but balances it with the fact that a person comes into this world with much of his or her design already in place. Therefore, people are ultimately responsible for their decisions in life, but their designs heavily influence who they are along with their directions in life.

LIKING WHO YOU ARE

The second benefit of assessment, which results from discovering who you are, is liking who you are. The recent deluge of emotional self-help books in the Christian marketplace is evidence that numerous Christians struggle with low self-esteem. In short, they have little knowledge of themselves and do not like what they do know about themselves. When they look in the emotional mirror they are not at all happy with what they see. The result is much pain and a constant search for pain relief.

Yet Scripture profoundly directs Christians to love themselves. In Matthew 19:19, Jesus commands, "Love your neighbor as yourself." Again, in Ephesians 5:28–29, Paul writes: "In this same way, husbands ought to love their wives as their own bodies. He who loves his wife loves himself. After all, no one ever hated his own

45

body, but he feeds and cares for it, just as Christ does for the church." Again, in verse 33, "However, each one of you also must love his wife as he loves himself, and the wife must respect her husband."

A critical factor in loving yourself biblically is to like yourself. The assessment process accomplishes this by tapping into the divine design and revealing what you are good at. It uncovers talents, gifts, leadership abilities, and many things of which you might be completely unaware. Then when they are employed in ministry, they provide a powerful sense of significance and delight to your soul.

BEING WHO YOU ARE

Awareness of the divine design sets off a chain reaction. Knowing who you are results in liking who you are. Liking who you are results, in turn, in being who you are. People who do not like who they are spend much time aping someone else. They are afraid that others will discover their real identity and reject them. This potential pain would prove unbearable, so they don masks and play roles to hide their identity.

However, when you discover who you really are in Christ and how God has uniquely designed each person in his image for a significant role in his kingdom, you become authentic. You can take off superficial masks, stop playing fictitious roles, and approach life and ministry in a fresh, vibrant manner. The Savior teaches that believers can know the truth, and the truth can set them free (John 8:32). The truth revealed in discovering their divine design frees Christians to minister without the barnacles of low self-esteem and past misinformation.

Organizational Value

How might assessment help ministry organizations in general and churches in particular? When the leaders and the people in a church discover their divine design, the ministry profits as a whole. Before going through the assessment process, the organization is like an eight-cylinder car hitting on three or four cylinders. However, after completing the process, it drives away a tuned machine hitting on all eight cylinders.

THE PRINCIPLE

Scripture is very clear that New Testament ministry is team ministry. First, Christ ministered in a team context. Being God he could have accomplished his ministry with a simple command. He chose, instead, to minister and pursue the Father's will through a small band of Palestinian disciples. He began by traveling and teaching from village to village calling the twelve to himself. This led to his sending them out two by two (Mark 6:7). Later, according to Luke 10:1, he appointed seventy-two others who were also sent out in pairs.

Second, Paul ministered through a team. Rather than attempt to fulfill the Great Commission mandate alone, he opted for a team. The initial team consisted of Barnabas and Paul (Acts 11:22–30). On the first church-planting journey, Paul added Mark to the team (Acts 13:2–3, 5). On the second, Silas (Acts 15:40), Timothy (Acts 16:1–3), Luke (Acts 16), and others (Acts 18) joined the three. Finally, additional people were added or used to form new teams (Acts 19–20).

THE PROBLEM

Reality teaches that people, even completely committed Christians, may experience difficulties and heartache in attempting to work together. This was true for the Savior, who was constantly disappointed by the disciples; he was even denied by Peter and betrayed by Judas. Eventually, before commencing the second missionary journey, Paul and Barnabas had a significant disagreement over whether or not to bring John Mark back on the team, because he had deserted them earlier. According to Acts 15:37–40, they agreed to disagree and pursue separate ministries. Interestingly, while Paul and Barnabas chose not to work together, they did not abandon the team concept (Acts 15:39–40).

In addition to personal problems between team members is the problem of placing the wrong person in the wrong position on the team. Every ministry team will experience differences of opinion. The problem is that some churches further exacerbate the problem by misplacing team members. We have all experienced the ecstasy of working on a good team and the agony of working on a bad one. As in athletics, it is critical that the right minister be put in the right position to make a good church team. As long as the quarterback plays his position, the team has a chance to win. If the coach decides to move his quarterback to offensive tackle, the results can be disastrous.

47

THE SOLUTION

One solution is ministry assessment. Scripture makes an analogy between the human body and the church (Rom. 12 and 1 Cor. 12). Just as the body has various parts such as a hand, an eye, and arms and legs, which are necessary for the body to function well in life, so the church is made up of different body parts that are crucial to the functioning of the body in ministry (1 Cor. 12:27). The purpose of a quality program of assessment is to help Christian hands discover that they are hands and to begin to function as hands and not as feet or toes.

The ministry organization such as the church determines what it wants to accomplish in a ministry. Then it recruits people who best fit by design the various positions on the ministry team. The result is fewer problems among team members and more efficiency in ministry. If an organization decides to plant a church, it looks for a church planter. If a plateaued or dying church wants to change its course and cast a new vision for ministry, it must find a change agent with a passion for reviving established churches.

The Purpose of Assessment

Experienced leaders are quick to acknowledge the truth that some pastors are better at leading churches than others. Furthermore, Lyle Schaller writes that the differences among churches affect the style of ministerial leadership that functions best for each congregation at its stage in life. He concludes, "These differences have also made obsolete the old cliché, 'Every minister should be able to serve any congregation.'"[2]

In 1 Corinthians 12, Paul affirms this basic principle: You cannot do anything you want to do in ministry. Contrary to the old cliché, some men simply were not designed by God to be pastors. Others were designed to be pastors and are good at church planting or church revitalization but not necessarily both. This truth underscores three specific purposes of assessment (figure 5).

To Discover a Divine Design

As discussed above, the purpose of assessment is to help Christians discover how God has uniquely designed them for their particular ministry (personal ministry identity). Several elements make up the divine design concept.

Figure 5
The Purposes of Assessment

Personal Ministry Identity Divine Design (Who Am I?)	Personal Ministry Vision Ministry Niche (What Can I Do?)

Personal Ministry Preparation Training Plan (How Do I Prepare?)

EVERYONE HAS A DIVINE DESIGN

The concept of God as master designer is reflected throughout all the universe. The psalmist writes, "The heavens declare the glory of God; the skies proclaim the work of his hands" (Ps. 19:1). This handiwork is evident not only in the beauty of the physical universe but in its design—the precise placement and circulation of the planets, the intricate structure of a leaf, and the circulation patterns of the winds and seas (Eccles. 1:5–7).

The animal world clearly reflects God's design, which is illustrated in the story "A Rabbit on the Swim Team":

Once upon a time, the animals decided they should do something meaningful to meet the problems of the new world. So they organized a school.

They adopted an activity curriculum of running, climbing, swimming, and flying. To make it easier to administer the curriculum, all the animals took all subjects.

The *duck* was excellent in swimming; in fact, he was better than his instructor. But he made only passing grades in flying and was very poor in running. Since he was slow in running, he had to drop swimming and stay after school to practice running. This caused his webbed feet to be so badly worn he became only average in swimming. But average was quite acceptable, so nobody worried about that—except the duck.

The *rabbit* started at the top of his class in running but developed a nervous twitch in his leg muscles because of so much makeup work in swimming.

The *squirrel* was excellent in climbing, but he encountered constant frustration in flying class because his teacher made him start from the ground up instead of from the treetop down. He developed

49

"charlie horse" from overexertion, and so only got a C in climbing and a D in running.

The *eagle* was a problem child and was severely disciplined for being a nonconformist. In climbing classes he beat all the others to the top of the tree but insisted on using his own way to get there.[3]

The lesson is clear. God created each animal with a unique design. He designed ducks to swim, rabbits to run, squirrels to climb, and eagles to fly.

The sovereign creator has brought each person into this world with a unique design as well. In Psalm 119:73, David writes, "Your hands made me and formed me; give me understanding to learn your commands." And in Psalm 139:13–14, David writes, "For you created my inmost being; you knit me together in my mother's womb. I praise you because I am fearfully and wonderfully made; your works are wonderful, I know that full well." God was the author and source of our spiritual makeup even before we came into this world. Jeremiah quotes God's word to him, "Before I formed you in the womb I knew you, before you were born I set you apart; I appointed you as a prophet to the nations" (Jer. 1:5). Other passages also hint at this design concept: Isaiah 49:1, 5; Luke 1:15; and Galatians 1:15.

EACH DESIGN IS UNIQUE

The story "A Rabbit on the Swim Team" illustrates that ducks swim and rabbits run. When ducks try to run or rabbits try to swim, they attempt to function outside their intended design, and serious problems soon develop.

While Christians may have similar designs, no two have the same design. Paul makes an analogy in Scripture between believers who make up the church, the body of Christ, and the various parts of the human body. In 1 Corinthians 12:17–18, he writes: "If the whole body were an eye, where would the sense of hearing be? If the whole body were an ear, where would the sense of smell be? But in fact God has arranged the parts in the body every one of them, just as he wanted them to be. If they were all one part, where would the body be? As it is, there are many parts, but one body."

A way to view this concept is to think of your design as God's "divine thumbprint" on your life. This image communicates two ideas. The first is the word *divine*, which teaches that God as creator-designer is the source of your design. The second is the word *thumbprint*, which implies uniqueness. While all thumbs are similar, no thumbprints are exactly alike.

The fact that God has sovereignly arranged all the parts of the body differently emphasizes the truth that Christians cannot serve God in whatever manner they please. An eye cannot serve God effectively as an ear, nor can an ear serve as an eye. This knowledge should save Christians from the "great assumption." Every year young men who have committed their lives to the Savior's service enroll at seminaries or Bible colleges for training to become pastors of churches. They do this with little thought as to whether or not God has designed them to be pastors. The implicit assumption, which is based on the American dream, is that you can do anything you want. Consequently, eagles try to swim and squirrels try to fly in the world of ministry. Both accomplish neither, which results in ministry burnout and in time ministry dropout.

EACH DESIGN HAS KEY ELEMENTS

Ministries are based on gifts, passion driven, poured through personalities, authenticated by character, and enhanced by natural talents or abilities. Therefore, to understand your design you must discover your spiritual gifts, passion, personality (temperament type), and natural talents or abilities.

The discovery of spiritual gifts is a good place to begin. A spiritual gift is a God-given ability for service.[4] The Bible lists spiritual gifts in 1 Corinthians 12–14, Romans 12, Ephesians 4, and 1 Peter 4. They include teaching, helping, exhortation, giving, leading, pastoring, administration, and others that are not contained in these four lists. These special gifts fuel the special abilities you need for ministry.

You may discover your spiritual gifts in two ways. First, study the biblical gifts and determine if you have a natural affinity for any of them. This method works best for those who are actively involved in ministry. Second, take one of the many spiritual gifts inventories which is available.[5] Spiritual gifts inventories provide a more objective approach to identifying gifts. Rather than choose one or the other, try both methods, and the results should prove enlightening.

Two steps give insight into the assessment of your spiritual gifts. The first is to understand your gift mix.[6] It consists of three to five gifts you demonstrate in ministry. My observation is that those with ministry experience display three to five spiritual gifts. At least two to three are fairly evident, while the others are less clear. The second is to understand your gift cluster. It includes all your spiritual gifts (gift mix) but emphasizes one that is dominant and supported by the others. For example, a professor at a seminary might have teaching as his dominant gift supported by the gifts of pastoring, administration, and helping. An evangelist's main gift would be evangelism supported by such gifts as preaching, leading, and exhorting.

Next, you should pursue your passion. I define passion as your God-given capacity to fervently attach yourself to some person or thing (a cause, idea, field of study, and so on) over an extended period of time to meet a need. It involves a fervent or strong emotional attachment. Someone describes it as "a burning gut feeling that a certain ministry is the most important place that God would have you." That passion has an object. It may be a person (the unchurched lost, the poor, the unborn) or it may be a cause (abortion, civil rights) or a condition (poverty, abuse, addiction). Not to be confused with a passing interest, passion stays with you over an extended period of time, and it often develops initially in response to a strong sense of need. Passion is important because it motivates and directs the activity of spiritual gifts. For example, a man with the gift of teaching may have a passion for teaching children who are victims of poverty in the inner city.

Once you have determined your gifts and passion, the next step is to determine temperament or personality. Two tools are helpful. The first is the *Personal Profile* (popularly known as the DiSC) which was developed by John G. Geier and Dorothy E. Downey as based on the earlier work of William Marston.[7] The acronym DiSC stands for the four behavioral temperaments: dominant, influencing, steadiness, and compliance. This tool analyzes behavior in nine specific areas: emotional tendencies, goals, criteria used in judging others, means used to influence others, one's perceived value to an organization, the tendency to overuse traits, typical reaction under pressure, fears, and what is needed to increase effectiveness.[8]

A second helpful tool is the *Myers-Briggs Type Indicator* (MBTI).[9] It determines how people conduct certain key functions. It focuses on four: extraversion vs. introversion (E or I), sensing vs. intuition (S or N), thinking vs. feeling (T or F), and judging vs. perceiving (J or P).

A fourth step that helps determine your design is to probe natural talents or abilities. They consist of creative expertise in leadership, administration, teaching, counseling, singing, playing an instrument, painting, drawing, acting, sculpturing, and many others. These natural talents differ from spiritual gifts (Eph. 4:7–13). Unbelievers have natural gifts from God, whereas only believers have spiritual gifts. Men such as Lee Iacocca and Sam Walton have demonstrated unusual natural ability to lead in their businesses. Should someone with the natural gift of leadership become a Christian, God may add the spiritual gift of leadership. This, coupled with some training and experience, could explain the ministries of some unusual people who have distinguished themselves as leaders in the Christian community.

To Determine a Personal Ministry Vision

Once you have discovered who you are (your divine design) you have an understanding of your ministry identity. The next step is to use this information to determine a personal ministry vision. Ministry vision focuses on your ministry niche. It is what God wants you to do with your life in terms of ministry. It answers the question, Should I be a pastor, a teacher, a professor, and so on? It also determines if a pastor should pursue church birthing, revitalization, or another area.

THE PROCESS

With a clear divine design in hand, determining a personal ministry vision requires examination of the various ministry areas and the design requirements of each. A few hints before you begin the process. First, seek out a person who has an expansive knowledge of ministry based on his experience and broad exposure to current ministries around the world. He will prove invaluable as a counselor. Second, determine if you already have an affinity for a ministry area in particular. If you find one, that is a good place to start.

There are several ways to proceed. One approach is to look at the various ministry positions and determine what designs are necessary for each. Then match your design with the positions that are options for consideration. For example, the position of a church planting pastor requires a design that includes the gifts of leadership and evangelism, a passion for both lost and saved people, and some combination of a D and an i on the *Personal Profile* (DiSC)

53

along with natural entrepreneurial or intrapreneurial abilities. If this matches your design, then church planting might be your ministry niche.

Another approach is to study the designs of individuals who have been successfully used of God in certain ministries for which you feel an affinity. For example, what components make up the divine designs of men who have successfully planted or revitalized a church? What are their gifts, passion, and temperaments? Then determine if their designs are similar to yours. If they are, pursue those similar ministries first. Attempt to find out as much information as possible about the men and their ministries. Visit with them and ask as many questions as possible. A final determiner would be a lengthy internship.

THE PROBLEMS

Several problems could surface before or during the process. The first is ministry vision in relation to the concept of a divine "call." Often, completely committed Christians agonize as they attempt to determine what God's will is for their ministry. Some describe this process as experiencing God's special, supernatural "call" on their lives. They spend much time on their knees praying and waiting for an experience similar to that of Isaiah in Isaiah 6 or Paul in Acts 9. However, these two experiences were unique to God's work in the lives of those men and do not appear to be normative.

Most often, God's will is to be found not in waiting for some special revelation but by studying both the Scriptures and how he has designed people. Therefore, those who desire to discover their ministry vision should spend much time with the Bible, which reveals his general will—how they should live, and so on. They should also detect his unique design in their lives, which reveals his personal will as to whether they should be a pastor, teacher, and so on.

Another problem is the need for significance. All Christians want to feel that what they do in this life is significant, that their lives are going to count for the kingdom, and that when they die the epitaph will read like David's: "For when David had served God's purpose in his own generation, he fell asleep" (Acts 13:36). They want the joy of knowing that they have served God's purpose in their generation.

Along with feelings of self-worth, a sense of ministry significance is important to your emotional health. If this is lacking in your ministry experience, you suffer adversely. The most obvious sign is ministry burnout. If the situation continues, the burnout will turn to ministry dropout. Therefore, determining your personal-ministry vision as based on your divine design is critical to the longevity of your ministry.

To Design a Personal Training Plan

Finally, personal assessment leads to the design of a personal training plan in preparation for your ministry vision. This plan includes a pattern and some possibilities.

THE PATTERN

Far too many completely committed Christians who pursue professional ministry start their preparation at the end rather than the beginning of the process. For example, in the past, men and women made the decision to pursue a seminary education after deciding on ministry as their vocation. This has changed. In the 1990s many students are using seminary attendance as a litmus test to determine if God wants them in full-time ministry. Thus a growing number of Christian professionals are working in the marketplace with a graduate theological degree.

This approach puts the proverbial cart in front of the horse. The order is critical. The pattern is important. But what is the proper pattern? First, you find out who you are (your personal ministry identity), which immerses you in the divine design phase. You discover your God-given spiritual gifts, passion, temperament, leadership style, and so on. Next, your personal-ministry identity serves as the foundation to develop a personal-ministry vision (what you can do). You ask, What ministries are clear options for me as based on my divine design? Affinity for a particular ministry and the advice from a mentor with ministry experience are practically a must at this level. Finally, when you have discovered your ministry identity and a ministry vision, you are ready to design a personal training plan tailor-made to help you realize your future ministry vocation.

THE POSSIBILITIES

The equipping plan includes several possibilities. The first, which most consider in an education-conscious society, is schooling. Schools provide the academics for ministry preparation. This is one of the reasons why God has raised up Bible colleges, Christian liberal arts colleges, and seminaries. The student armed with a clear sense of ministry identity and vision is in the ideal position to select the best curriculum and electives that will enhance his or her future ministry experience. This process should be extended beyond the seminary campus to include any seminars or conferences offered in your area during the years in school. This would include continuing education opportunities after graduation.

The second possibility is a must, not an elective. It is extensive experience in a church or parachurch organization that gives vital personal ministry experience. Most colleges and seminaries are weak in providing valuable ministry experience. They emphasize academics and the classroom experience. This has resulted in academic-oriented pastors and staffs with little actual "hands-on" experience.

The academic approach by itself is inadequate to equip men and women for leadership and ministry. Studies indicate that in the learning process the classroom is a distant third. Of second importance is learning from other people who serve as sources of guidance. Examples are the advice of a parent, a special teacher, or a coach. Number one is personal, actual experience.[10] Schaller observes that some of the megachurches realize this and have responded by discouraging their brightest, prospective pastors from attending seminary. Instead, they bring the most promising onto their staff and train them within the local church.[11] While seminaries go to the academic extreme, this goes to the practical extreme. We need both. Whether or not the seminaries and megachurches will be able to get together and resolve this problem is not clear. I suspect that the survival of the seminaries will depend on it. Regardless, the person with a clear ministry identity and vision is in a position to opt for both. One suggestion is to pursue seminary training and include a one- or two-year full-time, intensive internship in a high impact, quality ministry organization.

4

The Practice of Assessment
Are You a Change Agent?

The accusation was that Pastor Gary is a change agent. Like a prosecutor skillfully probing the accused for the truth, he has examined himself thoroughly in all areas of his divine design, and the jury has returned a guilty verdict. Consequently, he accepted the invitation to be the next pastor of Chapel Hill Community Church.

But exactly what process did he go through, and what did he discover about himself? As he worked his way through his assessment of this challenge, it gradually became clear to him that *who* executes change is as important as *how* it is done. Initially, he had numerous questions about *how* to lead churches through change. He has come to realize that the person *who* leads is as important, if not more important, than the process itself.[1]

This chapter purposes to help leaders and pastors determine if God has designed them to lead established, traditional churches to accomplish significant, planned change. It is based on several assumptions. The first is that some leaders are better at initiating change than others. In 1 Corinthians 12 and Romans 12 Paul teaches that you cannot do anything you please in ministry. The second is that the change will focus on the design of the primary leader or point person rather than the team. Actually, the ministry of a skilled, gifted team best accomplishes church revitalization. However, many plateaued or declining churches can afford only one full-time staff person. What does this skilled agent of intentional change look like? What are the spiritual qualifications, spiritual gifts, passion, temperament, and natural gifts and abilities that make up his profile?

Spiritual Qualifications

I believe that while spiritual (immaterial) qualifications are behaviors that God desires from Christians and not an aspect of divine design, they are essential to ministry as required in Acts 6:3–5. No two leaders have the exact same design; some are strikingly similar and some are vastly different. However, their lives are to be characterized by the same spiritual qualities. If God has designed a leader to revitalize churches, but the person does not demonstrate the necessary spiritual qualities, then he does not have the spiritual qualifications to lead any church. Therefore, the profile of a change agent begins with his character. Paul articulates the spiritual and character qualities for church leaders in 1 Timothy 3:1–13 and Titus 1:5–9.

Who are the leaders in the church? The character qualities of 1 Timothy 3:1–13 and Titus 1:5–9 relate primarily to pastors who hold the position of elder. A number of smaller churches are led by a full-time pastor and a board of several laymen. In many of these churches the lay board and often the pastor are designated elders. The Scriptures appear more accurately to assign the office of elder to those invested in ministry on a full-time, not a part-time basis. There are three reasons. First, the early churches that were led by elders were rather large in size. Their size necessitated a large staff or plurality of elders to direct the church's ministries. Second, the elders were responsible to shepherd their flocks (Acts 20:28; 1 Peter 5:2). To shepherd well takes a significant amount of time. The average part-time, voluntary lay person does not have the time necessary to shepherd a flock of people, hold down a full-time job, and meet the needs of his family. Finally, the elders were remunerated for their ministries (1 Tim. 5:17–18, 1 Peter 5:2). In fact, 1 Timothy 5:17–18 indicates that they were paid well whenever possible. However, this sounds very strange to the ears of today's churches that are run largely by lay elders. It does not appear to make sense, for many of them earn more money than the full-time pastor.[2]

What are the spiritual qualifications for leadership? J. Oswald Sanders divides the spiritual qualifications of 1 Timothy 3 into six areas. The first is social and is found in verse 2. He writes: "In respect to those within the church, the leader is to be *above reproach.* His character is to be such as will not leave him open to attack or censure."[3]

The second is a moral qualification. Sanders writes, "He is to be *'one wife's husband.'*" This means he must be blameless in his moral life and must "set a high standard in the marital relationship in his faithfulness to a sole marriage partner."[4] He adds to this category that "he must also be *temperate,* 'not addicted to wine.'" The idea is that he must never be drunk and disorderly.[5]

The third qualification is mental. He writes that leaders "should be *prudent,* soundminded." This refers to the inner character that is the result of a life of daily discipline.[6] Included in this same category is reference to an outer character that is *"respectable,* decorous." By this he means a well-ordered life that is the result of a well-ordered mind.[7] Also, the leader should be *able to teach,* which he describes as "a desire and constraint to impart to others the truth that the Holy Spirit has taught him from the Scriptures."[8]

The fourth is personality. Sanders writes that a leader must never be *"pugnacious,* but genial and *gentle*; not a contentious controversialist, but one who is sweetly reasonable."[9] Next, he says, a leader must be "hospitable, a friend of strangers," which he explains as extending hospitality to both Christians and non-Christians.[10] Finally, he combines *covetousness* with its twin, *love of money,* and explains: "The leader must never be swayed by considerations of financial reward. He is as willing to accept an appointment with a lower remuneration as one with a higher."[11]

The fifth is domestic. Sanders applies this in verses 4–5 to the married leader "who manages his own household well, keeping his children under control with all dignity."[12] He explains that ministers can spend so much time in taking care of the church and other spiritual matters that they neglect their families, their primary responsibility. The result is that they forfeit their right to lead the church.[13]

The sixth is maturity. This is a reference to the new or recent convert mentioned in verse 6. Sanders writes: "A recent convert lacks the spiritual maturity and stability essential to wise leadership. It is unwise to give key positions too early even to those who manifest promising talent, lest it spoil them."[14]

The leader who believes that God has uniquely designed him for church revitalization must be sure that he meets and maintains the qualifications outlined in this text. Many people in churches perceive change as an enemy. They resist it and often react adversely whenever and wherever it occurs. Therefore, they carefully study the character of their leaders to see if they are men of integrity. Any discrepancies found in those who attempt to lead them through the change process may lead to harsh criticism. Consequently, change agents must not only meet these qualifications initially but work hard at maintaining them consistently throughout their lives.

Spiritual Gifts

God has sovereignly chosen to bestow spiritual gifts on all those who are his spiritual children (1 Cor. 12:7, 11; Eph. 4:7). This fact alone should motivate you to discover your unique gift mix and how you best fit into his service. The knowledge of these gifts will contribute to the discovery of your ministry niche. They provide the tools of the change agent's toolbox. But what gifts have proved unique to change agents? How might a leader know if he has been spiritually gifted to lead a typical church through change? Several spiritual gifts naturally go with change and characterize persons who implement significant change in established churches. While the change agent should not expect to own all these gifts, the more he has the better.

Leadership

The first is the gift of leadership, identified in Romans 12:8. It is found in people who have a clear, focused vision and are able to communicate that vision to others in a way that influences them to become followers. This gift is necessary for anyone who desires to change churches, because it takes gifted leaders to move churches off plateaus or turn around declining churches. Usually these churches are without vision. They need a leader who can create dissatisfaction with what is (the status quo) and cast a vision for what could be. It is not the gift of administration and should not be confused with it.

Faith

The gift of faith is found in 1 Corinthians 12:9. It is the ability to envision what needs to be done and to trust God to accomplish it, even though such accomplishment seems impossible to the aver-

60

age Christian. Faith often clusters with the gift of leadership and is found in visionary leaders who ask, dream, and attempt big things for God (Eph. 3:20).

This gift is not the same as vision, but it enhances the visionary capacity of the leader. The gift of faith helps pastors want to revitalize their churches and to believe that change is possible. It aids in overcoming the fear of failure and convinces pastors to take risks for Christ's kingdom.

Exhortation

The gift of exhortation is listed by Paul in Romans 12:8. It is the ministry of encouraging, consoling, and when necessary confronting and admonishing others in the church so that the entire body is strengthened.

This gift is in high demand in churches enmeshed in the change process. Dying churches need daily encouragement and consolation. Churches that are plateaued and comfortable with the status quo need a certain amount of confrontation and admonition to begin to move forward again.

Mercy

The gift of mercy is also found in Romans 12:8. It is the capacity to feel and express unusual compassion and sympathy for those in difficult or even crisis situations. It seeks to provide distressed people with the necessary help and support to see them through the difficult times.

This gift is most helpful to pastors who work with declining churches. The church that is on the downside of the growth cycle may or may not be aware of its impending doom. People who recognize their fragile circumstances and stay often become discouraged and depressed. The gift of mercy provides change agents with a personal touch that brings hope and encouragement to these believers so that they are willing to give renewal their "best shot."

Preaching

The gift of preaching is not found in the three lists of gifts in the New Testament (1 Cor. 12; Rom. 12; Eph. 4). However, it is closely associated with the gift of apostle in 1 Timothy 2:7 and the gifts of apostle and teacher in 2 Timothy 1:11.[15] Preaching is the God-given ability to relevantly and persuasively communicate God's Word with clarity and power so that it has an impact on the lives of its hearers. Some equate the gift of preaching with prophecy.

Schaller writes: "One of the more highly visible methods of intervention in congregational life is the appearance of the skilled, persuasive, respected, influential, and effective leader who (a) has a vision of a new and different tomorrow, (b) can persuasively communicate that vision to others."[16] Pastors as change agents must be able to communicate effectively with their people. In fact, the casting of a significant, profound vision from the pulpit is a critical ingredient of change for established churches. If leaders cannot communicate their dreams for a better tomorrow, then their ministries will not see a better tomorrow.

Administration

The gift of administration appears in Paul's list in 1 Corinthians 12:28. It is the God-given ability to administer the affairs of the church. Good administration functions in three ways. First, administrators set goals and design plans and budgets to accomplish them. Next, they create an organizational structure around the plan and staff it accordingly. Finally, they monitor the plan and solve problems as they arise. This gift should not be confused with the gift of leadership, because Paul chose different Greek words and placed them in separate lists.

The gift of administration serves best in combination with the gift of leadership or abilities in the area of leadership. It allows change agents to both lead and manage well the ministries that are in process. It is not very effective, however, when there is no one with the ability or gift of leadership. And the change agent who lacks the gift of administration will need to find someone with this gift or find himself in great difficulty trying to cope with the very changes he has initiated.

Evangelism

The gift of evangelism is in Ephesians 4:11. It is the ability to communicate clearly the gospel of Jesus Christ to unbelievers either individually or corporately so that they come to faith in Christ.

A Christian who strongly desires to see lost people come to faith and pursues the same will have an impact on struggling churches in one of two ways. On the one hand, some churches are inspired by the efforts of those with evangelism gifts to implement a Great Commission vision. Their example is infectious. On the other hand, some churches become irate. All those new people around "who are not like us" pose a threat. Such churches prefer the status quo.

Passion

Spiritual gifts supply change agents with the tools or special abilities for their trade. Passion focuses and motivates those spiritual gifts. It is somewhat subjective, because its emphasis is on the emotions. Passion is a feeling that may be described as a burning, gut feeling that a certain ministry is the most important place that God would have you. In Romans 15:20, Paul uses the word *ambition* to describe his passion to proclaim the gospel to the Gentiles (v. 16). The leader must be careful to discern between passion and passing interests. Passion "sticks to the bones" in the sense that it is long-term. Passing interests come and go; they are here today and gone tomorrow. Passion stays with you for an extended period of time. Paul writes, "It has always been my ambition to preach the gospel." Some church planters acknowledge that they have wanted to be church planters for as long as they can remember. That is passion.

Therefore, passion becomes critical in helping pastors to determine if they are designed to pursue church revitalization. For example, men with and without significant pastoral experience who catch the vision for a Great Commission church are not sure whether to pursue church planting or church revitalization. The question is: Where is your heart? What does your heart whisper in your ear? What does that burning deep in your soul tell you? I have known several seminarians who had a passion for church planting but opted instead for a pastoral ministry in an established church because of various pressures to do so. Later they have confessed to me that all they think about is planting a church.

Leaders who are change agents for church renewal have a passion to minister to people in plateaued or declining churches. Like Pastor Gary, they have a special place in their hearts for people who have become disillusioned with the typical church and are going nowhere in their spiritual lives. They feel much like the Savior who, "when he saw the crowds, he had compassion on them, because they were harassed and helpless, like sheep without a shepherd"

63

(Matt. 9:36). They believe that in these situations they can make a difference and cannot wait for the opportunity to prove it.

Temperament

God-given spiritual gifts provide the special abilities for ministry, and a God-given passion supplies long-term direction and motivation for those abilities. However, God-given temperament provides unique personal character strengths for the ministry. As with spiritual gifts and passion, there are certain temperaments in pastors who are good at leading churches through change. Peter Wagner observes this when he writes:

> The fifth and final limitation on how strong a given pastor's role can be is highly personal. It depends on the temperament of the pastor himself or herself. Some pastors are take-charge people, and some could never bring themselves to take charge . . . I myself feel that each of us needs to regard ourselves as a product of God the Creator. He has not created every pastor for pastoring a large, growing church.[17]

Church-renewal pastors in the point position tend to display certain patterns on both the *Personal Profile* (or the *Biblical Personal Profile*)[18] and the *Myers-Briggs Type Indicator* (MBTI).

The Personal Profile

In his doctoral dissertation Robert Thomas used the *Biblical Personal Profile* to discover specific personality characteristics of effective revitalization pastors. He surveyed twenty Baptist General Conference pastors who, according to their various districts, "could turn a church around."[19]

Thomas described the ministries of these pastors as small, passive Baptist General Conference churches. He used the term *small* because the churches had fewer than 200 members. He used the term *passive* because they had experienced an average annual growth rate of less than 10 percent over the three-year period before the new pastor arrived. The evidence that they could turn a church around was the greater than 10 percent average annual growth rate these churches experienced over a period of time after the arrival of the change agent.

Upon completion of the pilot study, Thomas discovered that these effective revitalization pastors fell within the profile of the persuader pattern. He writes, "This pattern consists of a positive 'D' [dominant temperament] score of 5, a very high positive 'I' [influential temperament] score of 8, a negative 'S' [steady temperament] score of –11, and a negative 'C' [compliant temperament] score of –4" (see figure 6).

The persuader pattern is characterized by a high I in combination with a secondary D. I-type persons like to be around people and are articulate and motivational. They tend to generate lots of enthusiasm, enjoy participating in a group, and genuinely desire to help other people. They are risk takers who do not like the status quo and are "upfront," "out-on-the-point" kinds of people.

D-type persons want immediate results, love a challenge, and are catalytic. They tend to be quick decision makers who question the status quo, usually take authority, and are good at managing trouble and solving problems. They, like I-types, are risk takers who are task oriented and are "upfront," "out-on-the-point" kinds of people.

The persuader pattern results from bringing the high-I temperament together with a secondary D. The high I predominates, but the D also influences the temperament. What does this look like in an individual? The *Personal Profile* supplies the following description of the persuader pattern:

> Persuaders work with and through people. That is, they strive to do business in a friendly way while pushing forward to win their own objectives. Possessing an outgoing interest in people, Persuaders have the ability to gain the respect and confidence of various types of individuals. This ability is particularly helpful to Persuaders in winning positions of authority. In addition, they seek work assignments which provide opportunities to make them look good. Work with people, challenging assignments, variety of work and activities which require mobility provide the most favorable environment for Persuaders. However, they may be too optimistic about the results of projects and the potential of people. Persuaders also tend to overestimate their ability to change the behavior of others. While Persuaders seek freedom from routine and regimentation, they do need to be supplied with analytical data on a systematic basis. When they are alerted to the importance of "little things," adequate information helps them to control impulsiveness.[20]

In addition, the *Personal Profile* breaks down the persuader pattern into nine specific areas:

emotions	trusts others; enthusiastic
goal	authority and prestige; a variety of status symbols
judges others by	ability to verbalize; flexibility
influences others by	friendly manner; openness; verbal adeptness
value to the organization	seller, closer; delegates responsibility; poised, confident
overuses	enthusiasm, oversells, optimism
under pressure	becomes soft and persuadable; organized when desires to look good
fears	a fixed environment; complex relationships
would increase effectiveness with more	challenging assignments; attention to task-directed service and key details; objective analysis of data; collective perspective[21]

The value of Thomas's research is that either the *Personal* or *Biblical Personal Profile* can be used to help pastors determine if their designs are conducive to church revitalization. Ken Voges writes: "The Biblical Personal Profile (BPP) measures behavioral tendencies. It is not meant to be a prescriptive tool. You and others do not 'have to behave' like your profile. However, it is a fairly accurate predictive tool. You will 'tend' to behave as described."[22]

However, this raises the question, Are pastors with the persuader pattern the only ones who qualify to lead churches through change? Thomas has developed an operational or working profile for those who would use the Personal Profile to find revitalization

D i S C [segments]

	D	i	S	C	segment
28	+20	+17	+19	+15	6
27	+16	+9	+11	+7	
26	+15	+8	+10	+6	
25	+14	+7	+9	+5	
24	+13		+8	+4	
23	+12	+6	+7		
22					
21	+10	+5	+5	+3	5
20	+9	+4	+4	+2	
19	+8	+3	+3	+1	
18					
17	+7	+2	+2	+0	4
16	+5	+1	+1	-1	
15	+3	+0	+0	-2	
14					
13	+0	-1	-2	-3	3
12	-2	-2	-3	-4	
11	-3	-3	-4	-5	
10					
9	-4	-4	-5	-6	2
8	-6	-5	-6	-7	
7	-7	-6	-7	-8	
6	-8				
5	-9	-8	-8	-9	1
4	-10	-9	-9	-10	
3	-11	-10	-10	-11	
2	-13		-11	-12	
1	-14	-19	-12	-16	
	-21		-19		

pastors. This profile is one standard deviation off the mean of the qualified scores (see figure 7). He writes, "This would provide an 84 percent certainty that the qualified candidate would be included."[23]

This operational profile serves well as a starting place or a reference point for discovering leaders who are designed for church revitalization. The farther they move from this point in terms of their temperament, the less likely they will function well as change agents in the point position. I believe that a primary high D with a secondary I could lead a church as a change agent. Those, however, with a primary high S or a primary high C would serve better on a team with the high I or high D in the point position.

	D	i	S	C	segments
28	+20	+17	+19	+15	
27	+16	+9	+11	+7	
26	+15	+8	+10	+6	6
25	+14		+9	+5	
24	+13	+7	+8	+4	
23	+12	+6	+7		
22					
21	+10	+5	+5	+3	
20	+9	+4	+4	+2	5
19	+8	+3	+3	+1	
18	+7	+2	+2	+0	
17	+5	+1	+1	-1	4
16	+3	+0	+0	-2	
15	+1		-1		
14	+0	-1		-3	
13	-2	-2	-2	-4	3
12			-3	-5	
11	-3	-3	-4		
10	-4	-4	-5	-6	
9	-6	-5		-7	2
8	-7	-6	-6	-8	
7	-8	-7	-7		
6	-9		-8	-9	
5	-10	-8	-9	-10	
4	-11	-9	-10	-11	1
3	-13		-11	-12	
2	-14	-10	-12	-16	
1	-21	-19	-19		

The Myers-Briggs Type Indicator

I am not aware of any studies of the MBTI comparable to Thomas's studies of the DiSC. The MBTI is different from the DiSC and works with four categories of temperaments with which people function: extraversion or introversion (E-I), sensing or intuition (S-N), thinking or feeling (T-F), and judging or perceiving (J-P).

The first preference set (E-I) relates to where leaders focus their attention and derive their energy. Extraverts (E) like to work with the outer world of people and things. They are energized by contact with people. Introverts (I) prefer the inner world of ideas. They draw energy from solitude and find themselves drained if around a lot of people for a lengthy period of time. In *Personality Type and Religious Leadership*, Oswald and Kroeger conclude from a study of the functions normally expected in ministry "that the parish ministry is primarily an extroverted profession."[24] In my work with the MBTI and pastoral leaders, I have observed that God uses both E's and I's to lead churches that need strong direction and numerical growth. I would grant only a slight edge to extraverts.

The second set (S-N) looks at how people find out about things and how they prefer to take in and process information. People who take in information through the five senses (S) prefer to focus on observable facts and details—what they can see, hear, touch, taste, and smell. They tend to dwell on present reality (the here and now), and for them seeing is believing. Intuitive people (N) take in information holistically, preferring the world of ideas, possibilities, and relationships. They are the world's visionaries who thrive on change and new ideas. For them believing is seeing. These last two sentences indicate that change agents are clearly N's. Change agents must be strong visionary leaders who prefer the innovation that encourages growth in plateaued and declining churches.

The third set (T-F) relates to what people do with the information they take in, or how they make decisions. Thinking leaders (T) make their decisions on the basis of logic and objective analysis. They prefer to win people over by their logic. They take a more impersonal approach to decision making and can come across at times as insensitive. Leaders who pay attention to their feelings (F) make their decisions on the basis of personal values and motives. They prefer to win people to their ideas through persuasion. They take a personal approach to decision making and communicate warmth and harmony. Human values are very important; consequently they are more people oriented.

Various studies on change indicate that those who have a strong people orientation and are sensitive to people and their feelings and ideas are change agents. This is true of F-type leaders. The problem is they eventually stop exercising consistent strong leadership, which results in a church's plateau. This is not true of NT clergy.[25] T's and NT's in particular serve well as change agents because they are strong visionary leaders who press for change.[26]

The fourth set (J-P) reflects how people orient to the outer world in terms of structure and the time it takes to make decisions.

Judging-type leaders (J) prefer a more structured approach to life because they like to control and regulate life. They are very organized and deal with the world in a planned and orderly manner. Preferring to have matters settled, they tend to be quick decision makers. Perceptive leaders (P) take a less structured approach to life because they seek to understand and adapt to life. They tend to be very flexible and spontaneous. They have little need for closure and prefer to make decisions after all the facts are in.

The J's have an advantage in their ability to make hard decisions, take a strong stand, and commit themselves to a clear course of action.[27] However, when combined with the sensing type (SJ's), they can become very rigid and inflexible and prefer the status quo.[28] Consequently, SJ's do not serve well as change agents. The P's have an advantage in their openness to change, which brings both new options and a freshness to their leadership. However, their openness and flexibility often results in indecisiveness and failure to commit themselves to a plan for the future.[29] Consequently, either J's or P's can involve themselves in change but must work on the characteristics that inhibit their leadership toward change.

In working with type theory while at the University of California, Keirsey and Bates discovered that certain letters of the Myers-Briggs indicator combined to form four basic temperaments: NF, SJ, NT, and SP. This proves most helpful in discovering change agents. These four combinations can be placed along a continuum ranging from the most open to change on the left to the most resistant to change on the right. The NT's are on the far left while the SJs are on the far right. The SJ combination is the temperament most opposed to change. SJ's are traditionalists, the conservators and protectors of past values. They resist change and attempt to preserve the status quo. They make up 50 percent to 75 percent of most congregations, and their motto is, "If it ain't broke, don't fix it."[30] SJ clergy function best in a maintenance role. The NT combination is the temperament best designed for change. NT pastors are strong, visionary leaders who are agents of change.

Natural Characteristics and Abilities

Leaders who want to revitalize churches are wise to examine their natural characteristics and abilities. This section will focus on the characteristics, abilities, and circumstances of a biblical change agent—Nehemiah—who was used by God to lead the Jews in Jerusalem (who had survived the exile) through the difficult task of rebuilding the city walls. He models the skills and abilities of a superb change agent in a most difficult situation.

This list of abilities is not exhaustive, but they fall naturally into two areas. The first deals with leadership and the second with administration. Change agents rarely have all of these characteristics but should identify with some of them.

A Catalyst

Nehemiah was a catalyst for change when he led the Jews in Jerusalem during a dark period in Israel's history. He not only led them through change, he initiated much of that change. He was not a spectator but an initiator. He proved to be proactive, not passive. For example, he took the initiative to speak with King Artaxerxes about the tragic conditions in Jerusalem (Neh. 2:1–3), and he initiated the first contact with the Jews in Jerusalem (Neh. 2:11).

In *Discovering the Future*, Joel Arthur Barker discusses the characteristics of paradigm pioneers (change agents) and writes, "The paradigm shifter is a catalyst, a change agent, and part of the role of a catalyst is to stir things up."[31] Someone has to catalyze the change process, and change agents are designed expressly for this purpose.

An Outsider

Nehemiah was an outsider. When he heard about the desperate situation of the Jews who had escaped and survived the captivity in Jerusalem, he was living in Susa, located about 250 miles east of Babylon (Neh. 1:1). He came in from the outside and brought a fresh perspective to their situation. They had become immersed in their difficulties and accepted them as the status quo. Nehemiah viewed the situation from a different perspective and arrived in time to shake them out of their lethargy.

Barker asks, "What kind of person is a paradigm shifter?" He writes, "The short answer is simple: an outsider."[32] He explains that those leaders who come in from outside the present organization or situation lack investment in the old paradigm and thus have little to lose by creating a new set of rules.[33] This demonstrates the advantage of bringing in a new pastor as change agent from outside the church as opposed to promoting an assistant from within the ranks.

A Problem Solver

Nehemiah was obviously a problem solver. However, the problems were overwhelming. The walls to the city were broken down, and the gates were burned to the ground. Even more important was the Jews' emotional and spiritual response to their circumstances; they were in great distress and disgrace (Neh. 1:3). Nevertheless, Nehemiah did not back away from the problem. Instead, he attacked it and led these people in solving their problems. Barker in his discussion of a change agent (a paradigm pioneer) writes, "This person can best be described as a tinkerer. The key characteristic of tinkerers is that they fix problems that have become important to them."[34]

A Visionary

I have no doubt that Nehemiah carried a picture of the rebuilt walls and gates of Jerusalem in his mental wallet from the time God gave him the vision until all were in place (Neh. 2:17). Visionaries have the innate ability to see what others do not or cannot see. While they see needs, they have the natural capacity to see beyond those needs to the unique, exciting opportunities those needs present.

It is critical that leaders as change agents be visionaries. The visionary carries within his mind a snapshot of what the church will look like after it has progressed through the change process. Therefore, the leader knows where he is going and communicates a clear direction for the church. This enables him to cast a concise, focused vision to motivate his people to pursue the changes necessary to accomplish the vision. Lyle Schaller writes that a leader as change agent "(a) has a vision of a new and different tomorrow, (b) can persuasively communicate that vision to others, and (c) is able and willing to make the effort to win allies who will help translate that vision into reality."[35]

A Motivator

Nehemiah knew how to motivate people. In Nehemiah 2:17–18 he cast a strong vision in which he exhorted the Jews to rebuild the walls. In verse 18 they responded, "Let us start rebuilding." Consequently, change agents should look for the ability not only to cast vision but to motivate their followers toward the accomplishment of the vision. This becomes a never-ending process, for people have a natural attraction to the status quo. Once the change agent initiates the change, he must naturally motivate his people to continue the process, or they will to slip back into a status quo mentality.

A Persuader

Nehemiah knew both how to motivate and persuade people. In Nehemiah 2:4–8 Artaxerxes, after inquiring about Nehemiah's sad disposition, asked what he might want from him. The following speech, in verses 5–8, is a masterful example of how with God's help (v. 8) Nehemiah was able to persuade a pagan in a high position to be sympathetic to his cause. His persuasion was accomplished not by manipulation but by his godly example and history of service.

This ability to persuade has been discussed above in the section on temperament. In fact, Robert Thomas's research with the *Biblical Personal Profile* revealed that the persuader pattern best characterized pastors who had successfully led small, passive Baptist General Conference churches through revitalization.

A Risk Taker

There is no question that Nehemiah was a risk taker. When he appeared before the king with a sad presence (Neh. 2:1–2), he possibly risked his life (Esther 4:11). He also took a tremendous risk when he challenged the Jews in Jerusalem to rebuild the city walls (Neh. 2:16–17). There was no assurance that they would respond to his vision or follow his leadership. Why should they follow this outsider who materialized from nowhere? However, he took the risk, and God blessed the results with rebuilt walls and revitalized people.

In the chapter on paradigm pioneers, Joel Barker writes:

> Non-rational decision-making and courage: those are the two hallmarks of a leader. And can you think of any place where leadership is required more than the changing of paradigms? Leaders are willing to take a risk. This great risk, however, is balanced with

tremendous opportunity: if it turns out that the new paradigm is one with depth and breadth, those who change early have the first crack at all the territory.[36]

So while the change agent faces tremendous risk in challenging churches to change, there is a trade-off: the tremendous potential for being a part of something new and exciting that God initiates.

An Empathizer

As soon as Nehemiah heard of the Jews' tragic circumstance in Jerusalem he responded with great empathy and compassion for them. In fact, he spent a period of days weeping, fasting, and mourning for them (Neh. 1:4). This response revealed a heart of integrity that loved and cared about people. While they were to blame for much of their condition (Neh. 1:6–7), he did not castigate them but fell to his knees and petitioned God in their behalf (Neh. 1:8–11).

Men who seek to lead congregations through change should balance task orientation with people orientation. They need to love and sincerely care about the people whom they serve. Jesus Christ, the Good Shepherd, gave his life for the sheep (John 10:11). So must shepherds care deeply for their sheep. When their sheep hurt, they hurt; when their sheep struggle, they struggle.

A Perseverer

Nehemiah displayed an insatiable desire to persevere in spite of overwhelming odds. His ability to "hang tough" is most clearly demonstrated in Nehemiah 4:1–6:14 where he responded to the opposition party in Jerusalem who would greatly benefit if Nehemiah abandoned his vision. Most of the opposition came from Israel's unbelieving enemies (Sanballat, Tobiah, and Geshem) in the form of ridicule (2:19; 4:1–6), conspiracy (4:7–10), and rumor (4:11–12).

An ever-present distraction for change agents can be the temptation to quit. Some view opposition as a part of the challenge. The challenge to change minds and hearts is what pulls them into the situation to begin with. Others struggle more with opposition. The regular presence of unreasonable, misguided resistance from people within as well as outside the ministry (vision vampires and vision vultures) can eventually cause them great emotional and spiritual damage. There will be times when they want desperately to "take their marbles and go home." In their minds they may offer their resignation numerous times each day. However, they must not be "quick to quit." This does not mean that leaders of change do not come to a point where they may resign; some status quo situations are set in concrete. But this should not take place until they have given the situation their best effort over a reasonable period of time. The average tenure of pastors among Protestant denominations in America is 3.7 years. Yet it takes a minimum of five years for a pastor to gain the credibility to become the leader of a congregation.

A Planner

Nehemiah displayed administrative abilities as a planner. His response to King Artaxerxes (Neh. 2:6–8) reveals that he had a plan in mind prior to his risky encounter with the king. His inspection of the walls was a step in the plan for rebuilding the gates and walls of Jerusalem. The actual rebuilding of the walls (chap. 3) necessitated a carefully thought-out plan.

Change agents cannot walk into a church and instigate a revitalization program without a plan. Rarely does change take place where there is little or no preplanning. Therefore, they should discern if they have the ability to develop a workable plan or are in a position to work closely with someone who does.

A Recruiter

Nehemiah had the ability to recruit the allies necessary to implement his plan for Jerusalem (Neh. 2:17–20). This was wrapped up in his abilities as a vision caster (v. 17), motivator (v. 18), and encourager (v. 20). Without these people, he realized, there would be no rebuilding of the walls or gates of the city. Revitalization pastors cannot do it alone. They are dependent on the abilities of other leaders and workers to accomplish the task of rebuilding the church. Therefore, they must make an effort to regularly recruit allies to come on board and be a part of their team.

An Organizer

Nehemiah displayed his administrative skills as an organizer when the Jews began the building project (chap. 3). The text reveals that the families were well organized and assigned specific responsibilities. For example, Eliashib and his brothers worked specifically on the Sheep Gate (Neh. 3:1) while the sons of Hassenaah built the Fish Gate (Neh. 3:3). Agents of change need the administrative ability to bring together a number of different resources such as the people, funding, and equipment necessary to accomplish the dream. If they do not possess this ability, they must be quick to recruit someone who does.

A Delegator

Even the most careful reader of the Book of Nehemiah could miss it the first time through the book and if not specifically looking for it might miss it all together. It is the fact that Nehemiah did not rebuild Jerusalem's walls and gates. He was instrumental in the accomplishment of the project, but he did not nor did he even attempt to do it by himself. Chapter 3 and the following chapters are replete with the names of people who actually accomplished the work. Nehemiah was a delegator not a doer. He was a team player rather than a soloist.

Leaders of change in the twenty-first century cannot accomplish change on their own. It is critical that they develop a team of runners to whom they regularly hand off the baton of responsibility. Leaders who develop a plan and do not delegate its implementation to others but attempt it on their own are destined for frustration and eventual failure.

Part 3
The Practice of Change

Leading Established Churches through
the Process of Change

5

Why People Don't Change
The Change Resisters

We've never done it that way!" The words sounded familiar as Pastor Gary mulled them over in his mind. They are the infamous "six last words of the church," words that signal the beginning of a decline that culminates in "last rites" for most churches. They brought back painful memories of his experience as a lost seeker in the small struggling church he had attended during his college days. They represented the repeated response of the congregation whenever the pastor introduced any new ideas. That church is now history. He had not yet heard the words at Chapel Hill Community Church, but it was only a matter of time.

Past experience is a good teacher, and Pastor Gary has learned his lesson well. People, even Christian people, are allergic to change. The question is, Why? There are multiple reasons why people resist change. And the astute change agent had better be aware of the more common reasons if he is to lead a church successfully through the change process.

Felt Needs

Every man, woman, and child passes through this life with certain basic needs. However, it is their felt needs that demand action. Discover people's felt needs and you will know what gets their attention and dictates much of their behavior. Felt needs are the

keys that unlock the closed mind and touch even the most cal-
loused heart.

In most typical churches there are people who resist change
because they do not feel a need for change. If you asked them to
produce a list of their felt needs, you would not find change among
them. It is not a part of their working vocabulary.

Some of these people are not aware of all the change that is taking place around them. The wind of change has knocked their hats
off, and they do not know it. They do not realize that more change
has taken place in the last twenty years than in the last two thousand years. They are oblivious to the fact that more change will
occur in the decade of the 1990s than in the prior ninety years of
American history.

Others are aware that something is happening but they are not
sure what it is. They know things are not the way they used to be.
They often complain about the way things are. They do not like
what is going on, and they long for a return to the past. They yearn
for the good old days when life was a lot simpler.

More important, many do not have eyes to see how change is
impacting the church. They believe that all is well. They are not
aware that 80 to 85 percent of the churches in America including
their own are on a plateau or in decline. They do not realize that
the number of unchurched Americans is escalating to 60 percent
or more in the 1990s. They are oblivious to the significant growth
of certain cults and non-Christian religions all around them.

Consequently, they respond to any pleas for change with clever
slogans like, "If it ain't broke, don't fix it," or "We've never done it
that way." They sincerely believe that the state of the American
church is fine. If they had to assign their church a grade, it would
be an A or B. Others see problems but argue, "Simply leave well
enough alone and all will be fine." They believe their church needs
only to redouble its current activities: "We need more commitment
and to work harder." The problem is that they have assumed the
position of the proverbial ostrich. The head is buried deeply in the
sand while the rest of the large, protruding body is completely
exposed and vulnerable.

The solution is to help these people and their churches discover
that everything is not all right, that change should be found not
merely somewhere on their list of felt needs but near the top of

that list, that it should become a part of their working vocabulary. The hope is that they might become open to change or at least willing to give it a chance. Good leaders will lovingly lift the people's heads out of the sand, brush them off, and call their attention to the truth of what is taking place all around them. The Savior said, "You will know the truth, and the truth will set you free" (John 8:32). Truth has a liberating effect. The leader's greatest weapon in this situation is the truth which consists of the facts. The facts are that America is dying for change. The change agent must patiently and lovingly work with people until they begin to realize that the typical church in America is broke and in desperate need of fixing. Even though "we've never done it that way before," it is time to think in terms of new paradigms and to try new things.

But how do you accomplish this, especially with churched people in their fifties and sixties? Chapter 2 explains that the children of that generation largely make up the unchurched generation of the 1990s. The alert pastor of change will capture their attention and fuel a desire for change by pointing to the need for the kind of church that will reach their children and their grandchildren. He touches a felt need by asking, What would you be willing to do to reach your kids and your grandkids for the Savior?

The Status Quo

Many people in typical churches refuse to change because they prefer the status quo. Someone has said that their slogan is: "Come weal or come woe, our status is quo." When given a choice, they opt for remaining in their own private worlds as opposed to launching out into the public world of the unknown. They are comparable to the infant who prefers the comfort and safety of the mother's womb rather than a birth into a world of potential pain and discomfort.

To move out of one's comfort zone is not for timid hearts. Why is it so painful? Actually it is based not on reality but on people's perceptions of what life is like outside their comfort zones (see figure 8). It requires moving from a place of perceived safety (our world in here—"the womb") to a position of vulnerability (the world out there—"the enemy"). People are familiar with their present circumstances, whereas they do not know what lies "out

81

Figure 8
Comfort Zones

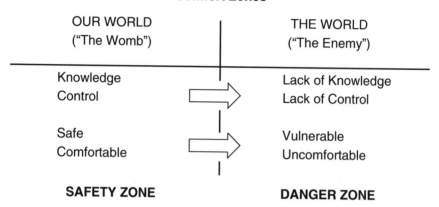

OUR WORLD ("The Womb")	THE WORLD ("The Enemy")
Knowledge Control	Lack of Knowledge Lack of Control
Safe Comfortable	Vulnerable Uncomfortable
SAFETY ZONE	**DANGER ZONE**

there." In their own comfortable world they feel that they have control over their lives. To move out of their comfort zones, however, is to give up that autonomy and be subject to another's control. Why would anyone want to risk that?

The status quo represents "what is" or "the way things are" in our churches. In most churches in the 1990s that is still made up of the forms and practices of the churches of the 1940s through the 1960s. If you want to know what church was like after World War II or the Korean Conflict, simply attend one of these churches.

This does not mean that the late 1940s through the early 1960s churches were wrong. Their forms and practices served them reasonably well for some forty or fifty years. Callahan identifies the problem in the following way:

> New understanding of doing ministry must be created with each new generation for the church's mission to move forward. When an older generation imposes its understanding on the new generation—however innocently—both groupings become dysfunctional. Each new generation must carve out an understanding of ministry that matches with its time.[1]

Values

Change agents as leaders must be aware that leadership always takes place within a context. In the marketplace this context is

82

called the corporate culture. In the church it is the congregational culture. The congregational culture consists of the traditions and values the church has acquired over the years of its existence. Lyle Schaller writes, "In the churches this may be described simply as 'tradition' or as 'the way we have always done things around here.'"[2] When a person in the church reacts to change with the slogan "We've never done it that way," he responds out of the congregational culture.

The primary motivating factor in its culture, however, is the church's values. Schaller writes, "The most important single element of any corporate, congregational, or denominational culture, however, is the value system."[3] What people value is most important to them. Along with their felt needs, values motivate people to activity or inactivity. Their values move them either to aggressively climb mountains or to casually look at mountains out the front window of their chalet. Some will even go so far as to die for their values. Patriotism is an example. Americans have voluntarily fought wars and given their lives because they value this country and that for which it stands. While church people may not die for their congregational culture, they will fight over it.

The term *philosophy of ministry* is used prominently in books on leadership, church planting, church revitalization, and others. Seminary professors and cutting-edge church leaders often punctuate their conversations with the term. The problem is that few people define it and many use it in different ways.[4] A church's philosophy of ministry is the core of values that govern its ministries. It explains *why* a church does *what* it does.[5] Most important, it represents the church's priorities and shapes virtually all its ministry decisions.

Pastors who desire to lead churches through revitalization need to accomplish two objectives regarding a philosophy of ministry. The first is that they must discover and understand their own philosophy of ministry so that they know their ministry values. These values affect them deeply and strongly influence their vision and leadership of the church. The critical question is, Does their philosophy of ministry line up with the church's philosophy of ministry?

The second is that they must know the church's philosophy of ministry so that they understand its ministry values. Schaller writes, "The values of any organization control priorities, provide the foun-

Figure 9
Four Responses to Change

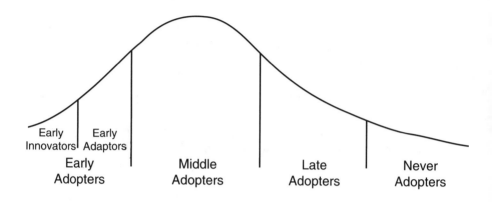

Early Innovators / Early Adaptors
Early Adopters | Middle Adopters | Late Adopters | Never Adopters

dation for formulating goals, and set the tone and direction of the organization."[6] The lesson to be learned is that the church's values as found in its philosophy of ministry have to be changed if the church is going to respond to change. Some pastors attend church-growth conferences put on by dynamic, high-impact churches. They study that church's programs and return to their church and attempt to replicate the same. This rarely works, because it assumes that the growing church and the church "back home" have the same values. The lesson is this: Change agents must change their church's values before attempting to change its programs. The key is to understand and change the plateaued or declining church's philosophy of ministry.

Vested Interests

People in traditional churches resist change because they cling to various vested interests. They make a strong commitment to Christ, which results in the investment of their time, talents, and treasure in the church and its programs. This is not wrong; in fact, it is what the Savior would have them do (Luke 9:57–62). It is most important that Christians commit themselves to various avenues of ministry and remain faithful to them.

Over a period of time, however, certain benefits accrue such as position, power, and prestige. An example is board leadership. Commitment to the church and its vision often results in an invitation to join the board, which in many American churches is a potential position of power and prestige. As the organization grows over a period of time, the power and prestige expand with it. This subtle process results in a need to protect one's investments, whatever they may be.

Change may mean the loss of power and prestige. Whenever a church changes from an old to a new paradigm, Joel Barker observes, "everyone goes back to zero."[7] He explains, "By zero, I mean that whatever leverage one had because of the old paradigm is dramatically diminished with the emergence of the new."[8] This poses a serious threat to those who have grown used to "having a say in what goes on around here." The result is a strong resistance to change based on the potential loss of power.

Other people in the church may also attain some power and prestige. A founding member may cast a lot of influence because of his or her faithfulness and contributions over the many years to the church. An affluent member who heavily supports the ministry may exert significant influence. Finally, a member may have begun a dynamic ministry in the church many years ago that has lost its impact. This person may still have some influence based on past performance.

The solution is to make every effort to win these people over to the new vision. The change agent needs to identify those in the church with vested interests and spend some one-on-one time with them to communicate the new vision for the church. Effective communication, or overcoming the problems of miscommunication, is half the battle. By focusing on these people, the change agent has an opportunity to make certain that the new direction is fairly represented and gets a proper hearing. For example, people who are in positions of influence on the church board need not drop out when a new paradigm comes in. The pastor of change takes the time necessary to cultivate and recruit each of them individually for his team so that they share ownership of the new paradigm.

Distrust of Leadership

Some people dislike change because they distrust those who would lead them through the change process. For example, older people, on the one hand, prefer leaders who have some experience and maturity under their belts. They find it most difficult to follow a leader whom they suspect is a novice—a recent seminary graduate, a pastor with little or no experience, a pastor without credentials, and so on. These people require pastor credibility before they will follow that leader.

On the other hand, younger people, and baby boomers in particular, project an antiauthority sentiment that appears to be the mood of the country once again in the early 1990s. They are not sure if they trust anyone in a position of leadership, whether that person is experienced or inexperienced. They have witnessed what they believe is a generation of leaders, political or religious, who have been inauthentic and seriously lacked integrity. In addition, they believe that they know as much about leadership as anyone else; therefore, they come across as unteachable. Consequently, they do not listen to change agents in the fields of church planting or revitalization because they believe they already know enough intuitively to accomplish these ministries on their own.

A significant number of people in every congregation question if they will be given a fair chance at change. Most often they are people who have been in the church for long periods of time and involved in its ministries. They are willing to entertain change but wonder about all the hard work that has gone into the church's past ministry history. Will the new leadership honor that past and provide a place for them in the church's future? If they believe that the leadership of change will not be fair and will not reward their sacrifices to change and develop new skills, they will not trust that leadership nor join its program of change. Therefore, leaders of integrity will recognize past accomplishments, honor people's commitments, and treat people fairly.

Godly character and integrity are the essential ingredients that qualify Christians to lead others in either the church or the marketplace. Leaders must realize that people today, both young and old, are asking two essential questions. The first is, Can you be trusted? Since character forms the very foundation of the ministry, a problem here affects the entire ministry. The 1980s proved a difficult time for those in ministry in light of all the moral defections on the part of those in high ministry positions. And there is no indication that this will abate in the 1990s. Those who successfully lead the church through the revitalization process in the future will be people who model Christ-like character.

The second question is, Do you know where you are going? This means ministry direction or vision. Thinking Christians are not so naive as to follow someone who has no clue as to where he is going. Astute church members want to know the leader's vision before they climb on board the ministry train. If they agree to involve themselves in the change process, then they have a right to know the direction of that change. Therefore, change agents who combine godly character with ministry vision offer ministry credibility, which attracts ministry followers.

The Stress of Change

Another reason people struggle with transition is stress. Much change has taken place in the 1980s. It is accelerating in the 1990s, and all evidence indicates that the pace will only increase in the early twenty-first century. For example, George Barna writes that in the field of information, "We now have only 3 percent of the information that will be available to us by 2010."[9] He also warns, "The gradual changes of the '90s—the result of three decades of ferment—will hit with full force by 2000."[10]

The problem for Americans in general and churched people in particular is change overload. People can only handle so much over a short period of time. Alvin Toffler has warned that to subject people to too much change in a brief span of time results in future shock or shattering stress and disorientation. Commenting on this, Ken Gangel writes: "Toffler's theories, written more than a decade ago, seem to have been prophetic. The rapidity of change actually makes people sick. They no longer feel certain of anything—job, spouse, beliefs, morality—everything seems to be changing all the time. A pervasive uncertainty hangs like a fog over everything in the modern world."[11]

In light of the dizzying pace of rapid change taking place in the world out there, people look to the church as a place of safety and protection from the shattering stress of change. The church represents the one place where they can go to get away from it all, to pause and regain their composure. The church is the only thing in their lives that does not change and provides them with a certain amount of stability. Every Sunday they come in from the disarming world of shattering change to a place that looks and acts the same week after week, year after year. They know what to expect, and there are no surprises. Consequently, to attempt to change what has become an island of stability is most threatening.

The problem is that the church that fails to change fails to impact the culture of change. It becomes a dinosaur, a memorial to a world that no longer exists. So, on the one hand, while it protects those within its walls from overwhelming stress, on the other hand, it becomes biblically and spiritually irrelevant. That which is to be the salt of the earth turns tasteless, and its light flickers dimly if at all (Matt. 5:13–16).

How can a church implement planned, positive change and remain a bright light and savory salt in the community? There are several steps an agent of change can take to alleviate some of the stress. One is communication. As much as possible make sure people are kept informed of what is taking place. While some may resist the direction of known change, they resent most of all not being informed of that change. They believe the leadership is trying to hide something from them; this makes them very suspicious, which breeds distrust—the achilles heel of leadership. Communication is one of the tools of change explored more fully in chapter 9.

Another step to alleviate stress is assurance. Members who are followers of change agents need assurances from trusted people that the proposed changes are in the best interests of the church. Thus a word of testimony from a credible source who has experienced a similar change in another situation provides the encouragement and assurance necessary to calm troubled spirits.

A third step is to encourage participation in the change process. There is a big gap between being the initiator of change and being the recipient of change. One is active while the other is passive. Those on the active side exercise some degree of control, and those on the passive side see themselves as vulnerable. Therefore, leaders of change should attempt to involve their people wherever possible as active agents in the program of change, to mobilize a lay army of fully devoted disciples. Chapter 10 develops this topic.

Differences of Temperament

An important aspect of a person's divine design is his or her temperament. As covered in chapter 3, each person comes into this world with a unique design from God. This design consists of certain natural talents and abilities, passion, leadership style, and so on. When a person accepts Christ, God adds to that design certain spiritual gifts (Eph. 4:7–13). A critical area of design for both believers and unbelievers is temperament, and temperament is another reason people in churches resist change.

People who are often found on the cutting edge of change are of high dominance temperament, as are also those of highly influential temperaments. Both generate lots of enthusiasm, enjoy participating in a group, genuinely enjoy helping other people, are risk takers who do not like the status quo. Thus they are initiators of change by design, prefer a climate of change, and handle it well.

Sensitive temperaments emphasize steadiness or stability. For them, change turns secure situations into insecure situations and their tendency is to resist change.

The ideal environment for compliant temperaments includes security assurances, standard operating procedures, a sheltered environment, no sudden or abrupt changes, maintenance of the status quo, assurance of quality control, and people who call attention to their accomplishments. Consequently, they, too, resist change.

The solution focuses more on people with high-S and C temperaments than the high-D and I temperaments. The latter usually functions well in times of intense change and even may be the source of it. This is not true of the high-S and C temperaments. However, high-S persons can cope with change. The fact that they are designed to be good listeners and to calm excited people is a definite asset in the change process. While they prefer the status quo, they will embrace change if given substantial reasons for it.[12] Consequently, the change agent who carefully communicates and explains the changes he implements will win the favor of these people.

People of high-C temperament can also cope with change. Their desire for excellence in quality can serve to enhance the quality of change. Good leadership knows the importance of excellence in ministry, and a vital aspect of excellence is quality. Those with high-C temperaments will embrace change if they are given assurance of quality control.[13] Most often a status quo ministry is synonymous with low quality. Helping a high C to realize this encourages him to support and be involved in quality change. Therefore, the desire for quality found both on the agenda of the change agent and of the person of high-C temperament can help them work together to enhance the change process.

Another way to use it is through the *Keirsey Temperament Sorter* described in chapter 4. People with the NT temperament make up about 12 percent of the population.[14] They are visionaries and good conceptualizers who look ahead to the future where they see exciting possibilities. However, they appear insensitive at times because of their task orientation and may have a problem following through on their projects—they are quick to abandon boring routines. Being very innovative, they are most open to change. The key is to appeal to their intellect and to involve them in the change process.[15]

The SP temperament is found in 31 to 38 percent of the population.[16] They are independent, free spirits who focus on the facts and realities and will "tell it like it is." They are especially good at handling crisis situations because they long for action and excitement and are risk takers. However, SP persons can be unpredictable and impulsive. They become bored when there is no crisis to solve and may create one to have something to do. Consequently, they opt for change in an unplanned crisis context. In other situations, involving planned change, they are neither a positive nor a negative force for change.[17]

People with the NF temperament make up approximately 12 percent of the population.[18] They are sensitive, generous people who focus on meaningful relationships. They have good verbal and listening skills and are most effective at getting people to work together to achieve the ministry's goals. They are people oriented and struggle over giving too much of their time. They are taken advantage of and easily hurt. NF's are important to the change process, because institutional change will not occur without their support. They will opt for change if it meets the needs of the people in the congregation but not sudden changes.[19] The skilled change agent will either leak information to them or make sure they have any proposed changes well in advance of their implementation.

Finally, the SJ temperament is found in 38 to 45 percent of the population.[20] They are the decisive, practical realists who focus on present facts and value the past. They are the maintainers of the church's traditions who desire to preserve meaningful church institutions. They pay strict attention to policies and regulations, are organized, dependable, like to work, and can be counted on to finish what they start. The SJ is the most resistant to change. Keirsey and Bates write the following:

> Providing SJ with *facts* to support a desired change may help to engage their cooperation. Furthermore, if the desired change can be described in terms of a more efficient way of getting things done, in terms of a better procedure, the SJs will be likely to react positively in the degree the change makes sense to them. In contrast to the NFs, who need verbal discussion, the SJs need to have written documents describing the change. In fact, they tend to become rather impatient with discussions, particularly repetitive or lengthy discussions. If the SJs can be involved in writing a procedural manual involved in the change, they are apt to be delighted and are also apt to produce a thorough and sensible document.[21]

The leader who desires to be a skilled, respected change agent is wise to become a student of temperament. He should study both the *Personal Profile* or the *Biblical Personal Profile* (DiSC) and the *Keirsey Temperament Sorter* and become adept at their use.[22] Proficiency in the use of the *Myers-Briggs Type Indicator* (MBTI) is preferable; however, adequate training is both costly and time consuming.[23] Instead, the *Keirsey Temperament Sorter* is a good substitute. The change agent should purchase a copy of *Please Understand Me*, study it carefully, and use the KTS provided in the book.[24]

Sacred Cows

A seventh reason churched people resist change is the sacrosanct. In *Say No, Say Yes to Change*, Elaine Dickson writes: "We give some things a sacred quality although they are not intrinsically sacred. Some things become our 'sacred cows.' Whatever is considered sacred—genuine or not—becomes relatively immune to change."[25] National examples are The Star-Spangled Banner and the American flag. Consider the uproar caused by the burning of the flag or a different rendition of the national anthem.

Over the years churches nurture and milk their own sacred cows. In the process of fleshing out various biblical principles, they elevate the forms of those principles to positions of special stature. Eventually the form is confused with the principle and the former is valued as highly as the latter.

The typical church is replete with examples. The church's music during the worship hour must consist of the great old hymns of the faith accompanied by an organ. Anything else is less than sacred. The King James Version is the only Bible that is read on Sunday mornings. As one parishioner says, "If it was good enough for Paul, it is good enough for us." Everyone knows that a committed church has a minimum of three meetings a week: the Sunday morning worship service, a Sunday night preaching service, and the Wednesday night prayer meeting. One saint expressed it this way: "You can tell how many people love the church by those who are faithful on Sunday mornings. You can tell the people who love our pastor by those who show up Sunday evenings. But you'll discover those who love the Lord by the faithful few who come to prayer meeting every Wednesday night." Other sacred cows may be the order of worship, King James Prayers, the length of a Christian's hair, and even the name of the church.

The way to deal with this is through sound biblical teaching. The leader of change who is an expositor of the Scriptures should take great pains to make a clear distinction between the eternal, unchanging principles of the Bible and the various forms those principles take. The solution to confusing a practice with a principle is not to let people confuse the two in the first place.

Those who already have a herd of sacred cows grazing on the church's front lawn can be politely and lovingly challenged in private. For example, the change agent could visit at home the member who insists that Scripture be read on Sunday mornings from the King James Version and invite him to justify his view from the Scriptures. While he may not change his opinion overnight, chances are good that he will not express it in public with the change agent present.

The Complexity of Change

Someone has said that "you can only be sure of two things in this life: death and taxes." We can be sure of many things, one of which is that life itself will only become more complex.

One of the byproducts of good leadership is change, which in turn creates much complexity. Strong, entrepreneurial leaders like Andrew Carnegie and Pierre Du Pont created vast enterprises which grew and became more complex. In response to this growth, management developed to help these businesses function on time and on budget.[26] While good leadership produces change and complexity, good management helps an organization cope with all that change and its complexity.

Strong biblical leadership in the American church will also produce significant, positive change that results in much complexity for the members of the church. The natural tendency is to resist the complexity by opposing the change. The logic is that complexity can be confusing and disruptive; therefore, resist the change and eliminate the source of complexity. If enough people follow this logic, they will stifle effective leadership and dull ministry momentum. In time the church will plateau and the leadership will hear God calling them to graze in greener pastures.

The solution is to balance good management with good leadership. Then as leaders implement the various changes necessary for effective ministry, the managers of change work with them to bring order out of complexity. Effective ministry requires an individual or team of individuals with both leadership and management capabilities. Consequently, the church must take responsibility to recruit and enlist these kinds of people.

Ideal for smaller churches led by a single pastor is someone with a balance of strengths in both leadership and administration. Most people can be found somewhere along the leader-manager continuum. On one end is the pure leader who has virtually no management abilities. On the other is the pure manager who has few capabilities in the area of leadership. In reality most persons are not at either of the extremes but are somewhere in between. The challenge for the smaller church that desires to maintain the momentum of change is to find a leader who is close to the center of the continuum.

93

The Paradigm Effect

Joel Arthur Barker believes that paradigms act as physiological filters through which people see their world.[27] He writes, "What may be perfectly visible, perfectly obvious, to persons with one paradigm may be quite literally invisible to persons with a different paradigm."[28] Barker was influenced by Thomas Kuhn's *The Structure of Scientific Revolutions*. He quotes Kuhn:

> In a sense that I am unable to explicate further, the proponents of competing paradigms practiced their trades in different worlds. . . . Practicing in different worlds, the two groups of scientists see different things when they look from the same point in the same direction. Again, that is not to say they can see anything they please. Both are looking at the world, and what they look at has not changed. But, in some areas, they see different things, and they see them in different relations one to the other. That is why a law that cannot even be demonstrated to one group of scientists may seem intuitively obvious to another (p. 150).[29]

What is true in the world of the scientist is true in the world of the church. What may be perfectly visible and obvious to some members who view the church through one paradigm is invisible to others who see the church through another paradigm. They both view the same situation but receive different information because their lenses (paradigms) are different. Therefore, some are able to perceive clearly what is actually happening in the church and the world around them and some cannot. The problem is that their paradigms, right or wrong, are the sources of their values, attitudes, and ultimate behavior and relationships in the church.

There are several ways to deal with this. One is to help people understand the paradigm effect. An assumption that everyone sees the same things in the same way only results in increased frustration and ministry obsolescence. An explanation of paradigm helps people and churches realize and understand their differences. Then they are in a position to redefine their paradigms and embrace new approaches to ministry. One aid to leaders and congregations is Barker's excellent video *Discovering the Future*, in which he shows numerous, indisputable examples of paradigm shifts in the world in general.[30] Follow this video with a discussion on paradigm shifts in the church in America and your church in particular. As people become more aware of the influence of their paradigms, the more they are willing to discuss them and reexamine them in the light of objective reality.

Also helpful is to provide people with accurate information about their world. Since paradigms are filters through which people see the world and the church, leaders affect change by regularly presenting a different, more accurate picture of that world and the church. One way to accomplish this is to present the information in chapter 2. Most people are unaware that the traditional American church is in deep trouble, that the majority of Americans are unchurched, and that we are living in a post-Christian era. When this information becomes a part of their paradigm, they are in a position to consider powerful changes in their churches.

Do not overlook the effect of crises that take place in the life of the church and the individual lives of its people. A crisis has the greatest potential to initiate change in the life of the church.[31] A crisis such as a fire, the loss of a pastor, or a church split affects the entire church. Individuals experience personal crises of accident, death of a loved one, and so on. When people face these crises, they are forced to see life from a different perspective and experience a fundamental shift in thinking, which results in a paradigm shift. And it is these basic paradigm shifts that lead to change in churches. While change agents can engineer some crises, they need to develop "crisis-sensitive eyes" to spot potential crises and use these God-given opportunities to accomplish paradigm shifts.

Self-Centeredness

I have observed that discussions about why people refuse to change seldom mention self-centeredness. When I ask certain church members why they refuse to entertain a proposal for change, no one ever gives selfishness as the reason. Reality is that some people look out first for themselves. This is evident in two areas. First, a "meet-my-needs" mentality is evident in the church as well as the world. To expect the church to meet needs is legitimate. The Jerusalem Church ministered to people's needs (Acts 2:44, 45; 4:34–36). However, some people are concerned only with their needs and not the needs of others. They suffer from "nearsightedness." They desperately need to take the next step and minister to the needs of others. On an institutional level, this means change. For example, a church may never reach out to the non-Christian people in the community because its people are too busy pouring their money and time into building programs and other programs for themselves. A new pastor's attempts to implement a community evangelism program or an inner-city soup kitchen will be met with strong resistance.

Another area of evident self-centeredness is control. As I grew up, I observed that in many ways life is all about being in control and not allowing others to control you. This is wicked and selfish. It starts at a young age. For example, as children, people try to manipulate their parents by crying and misbehaving to get their way. During the teen years, they attempt to control what others think about them through such things as involvement in athletics, accomplishment in academics, and so on. In adulthood, they take pride in their spouses, homes, kids, and church. They look at them and assure themselves that they are, indeed, in control of their lives. In effect, they are using control as a means to intensify a sense of esteem. In doing so, they ignore selfish behavior and attribute any self-serving motives to others. In the church, when someone introduces change, it often poses a threat—it means the potential loss of control over someone or some program, and, in turn, a loss of esteem. The natural thing to do is to resist that change. And the greater the change, the greater will be the resistance.

The ultimate source of all this is the flesh or sinful nature. In Galatians 5:16–17 Paul writes, "So I say, live by the Spirit, and you will not gratify the desires of the sinful nature. For the sinful nature desires what is contrary to the Spirit, and the Spirit what is contrary to the sinful nature. They are in conflict with each other, so that you do not do what you want." The problem is that while many believers in the church are aware of this truth, they seldom apply it to their situations. Paul writes that the sinful nature is very deceptive (Rom. 7:11; Eph. 4:22). People who resist constructive change for selfish reasons often manage to convince themselves that their concerns are spiritual not carnal. They believe all that the flesh whispers in their ears.

The solution is for God's people, both leaders and followers, to regularly examine their hearts (2 Cor. 13:5). They must examine in particular the motives of their hearts. Why do they resist a particular change? Is it based on love and concern for the church and its vision or on their own personal agenda? The answer lies more in how they disagree rather than in what the disagreement is about. Does disagreement express care and concern for the leader who proposed the change initially? Ultimately is everyone on the same team?

6

The People of Change
Who Votes For and Against Change

Pastor Gary had carefully worked his way through a checklist noting some of the reasons why the people at Chapel Hill Community Church might be resistant to change. He admitted that this was a little premature; while he had accepted the position of pastor, he was not yet on the scene. Therefore, any conclusions might prove inconclusive. However, he believed in being proactively prepared, a vestige from his Boy Scout days combined with his temperament. Pastor Gary had decided to walk through the front door of the church with a preplanned program for change. A knowledge of why Chapel Hill people might resist change would be vital to that plan. He acknowledged that it would be modified considerably, but a plan in hand is better than no plan at all.

Next, he began to think about the people at Chapel Hill with whom he had come in contact. He had been at the church as a candidate several times and made a point of meeting as many people as possible. He had even requested to visit with them in their homes, especially the leaders. He probed with seemingly innocent questions designed to reveal where people stood on the issue of new ideas and possible change. His purpose was twofold. The first was to discover who might be open and who would be resistant to proposals for change. The second was to find out who the opinion makers were. Pastor Gary was gaining a body of knowledge about his people that is vital for any skilled change agent. It consists of two major parts.

Part 1: The Categories of Change Response

When a leader introduces change into a church's ministry, the people will generally fall into four categories according to their response: early adopters, middle adopters, late adopters, and never adopters, represented on the bell curve in figure 9, p. 84.

Early Adopters

Veteran change agents have discovered that when they introduce a new idea or proposal for change, there will be those in the ministry who jump on board almost immediately. These early adopters fall into two groups.

EARLY INNOVATORS

The early innovators make up approximately 2 to 3 percent of most established congregations. They are people who exist at the outer fringe of change. Early innovators are the real pioneers or originators of new ideas. They are highly creative dreamers who see all kinds of possibilities for the ministries of the church. Their tendency is to focus more on the cognitive than the practical aspects of the ministry. Thus they talk a lot about innovation but are not good at implementing it. They enjoy exploring various theories and ideas for ministry but are found toward the rear if the ministry ever becomes a reality.

Early innovators are one of the most frustrated groups in the church. They see lots of potential for the church in America but feel that it may never be realized unless something unusual happens. The problem is that they find themselves in churches that are much the opposite. They have suggested numerous ideas for change only to hear, "We've never done it that way." When the church has adopted their ideas, Win Arn notes, they seldom receive credit for them.[1]

Many early innovators fall within the creative pattern on the *Personal Profile*. The *Profile* describes them as somewhat restrained emotionally and willing to accept aggression. Their goal is unique accomplishments and dominance. They judge others by their progressive ideas and influence others by setting the pace in developing a system. Their value to the church is in their abilities to initiate and design change. They have a tendency to overuse bluntness and display a critical or condescending attitude. They fear inability to influence others and failure to achieve their standards.[2]

100

In general the church has turned a cold shoulder to them. It views them as different and has grown tired of entertaining all their "weird" ideas. If these early innovators have been in the church for any length of time, they have probably given up and become attenders or inactives. This response has served only to damage their credibility in the eyes of the active members. Therefore, they have little clout.

EARLY ADAPTERS

The other group of early adopters are the early adapters, who make up 8 to 18 percent of the church. They have grown tired of the status quo because they have watched it sap the church of its vitality. Thus they are open to change and are looking for new ideas for the church. However, Ellis writes: "They are willing to try a change that promises progress. They are not necessarily impetuous, but are sensitized to the idea of change and respond to an opportunity quickly."[3] They are quick to spot a good idea when they see one, but often get credit for the ideas of the early innovators.

While early adapters are found in all four temperaments (DiSC) of the *Personal Profile*, a significant number are high D's and high I's. In general, this is because the high-D people function best in an environment where there is opportunity for individual accomplishments, a wide scope of operations, freedom from controls and supervision, and many new and varied activities.[4] High-I persons perform best in an environment where there is freedom of expression, freedom from control and detail, and opportunities to verbalize their ideas.[5] On the *Keirsey Temperament Sorter*, both early innovators and early adapters are primarily NT's and SP's in a crisis situation.

Ellis recognizes other characteristics as well. He writes that they "tend to be younger, better educated, less provincial, more well-traveled, more likely to participate in numerous activities, more active in seeking information, and less rooted in the existing system."[6]

Early adapters tend to be frustrated in the typical, traditional church. But they are optimistic and dream of a better tomorrow. In general, most congregations like them and get along with them; it has to do with their youthful enthusiasm. In fact, they are active in the life of the church and usually gravitate toward various leadership positions in the ministry. While the congregation respects them, they are slow to adopt their ideas and implement the changes they suggest.

APPLICATION

A key church revitalization principle is to recruit as many active, vocal allies as possible for your program of change before you introduce it to the congregation. Schaller indicates that one characteristic of a leader who can intervene in the congregational status quo and initiate change is the ability and willingness "to make the effort to win allies who will help translate the vision into reality."[7]

The change agent should seek out the early adopters as his allies and rally them behind his programs and proposals. Actually, finding them will not be too difficult, because early adopters quickly gravitate toward the new leader of change. The strategy is to move the people who are spiritually qualified into positions of high leadership in the church such as the board and various influential committees.

However, this may prove difficult, because they are often the younger members of the church who have not yet attained the necessary credibility and seniority. Most likely, they are the same age or are younger than the new pastor and have joined the church at the same time or after his arrival. However, Schaller gives some encouragement: "Every history of organizations, institutions, and nations reveals that major changes are initiated by a tiny minority, not a majority. The only exception . . . is when a widespread perception of crisis exists."[8]

Never Adopters

If the four categories of change response are placed along a continuum from those people who are most likely to respond to change on the left to those who are least likely on the right, the early adopters would be on the far left (see figure 10). On the far right are the never adopters. Both groups serve as bookends or the two extremes that represent the contrasting attitudes toward

Figure 10
Continuum of Change Response

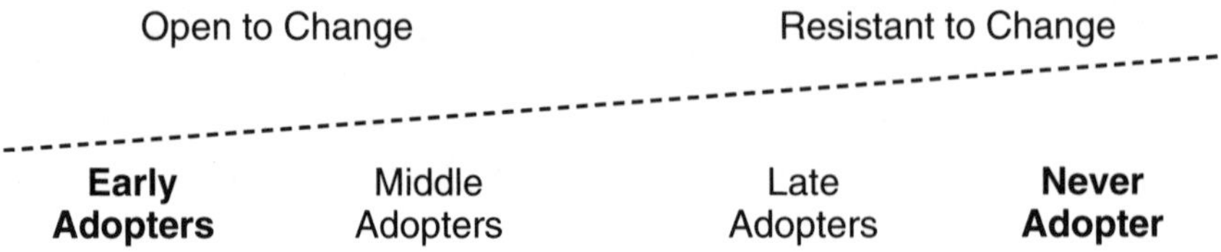

Open to Change		Resistant to Change	
Early Adopters	Middle Adopters	Late Adopters	**Never Adopter**

change in a typical congregation. Each bookend exerts influence for or against change from its end of the shelf.

The never adopters are the laggards or strongest resistors to change and make up from 2 to 20 percent of the long-established church. A typical never adopter is the deacon who walks into a meeting late, realizes that a vote is taking place, and says, "I don't know what you're voting on, but whatever it is I'm against it." Chances are good that these people will never vote for change. Rather than adopt new ideas and proposals for change, they openly resist them. They are solidly committed to the status quo "come hell or high water." The never adopters sincerely believe that they can recreate yesterday if they only hang on to *what is* long enough. They can be persistent, negative, and obstinate. At their worst they may be divisive or even attempt to split the church (1 Cor. 1:11–17).

From the standpoint of temperament, they are found in all four temperaments of the *Personal Profile*—D, i, S, or C. However, there are more S's and C's simply because these temperaments initially prefer the status quo. They are primarily SJ's on the *Keirsey Temperament Sorter*.

People assume that all the never adopters are traditional churched people in their fifties and sixties. While the majority are those of the FDR generation rather than the Pepsi generation, there are representatives of the boomers among the never adopters. They are the young people who were born into the long-established churches and opted not to drop out. They have grown up in the context of older, traditional forms and value them.

The never adopters exert more clout in the church than the early adopters. There are several reasons. One is that they are usually older than the early adopters. Therefore, they are in a position in life to have accumulated enough finances to contribute significantly to the church's budget which gets everyone's attention— especially of those on the board. In addition, their age and experience grants them seniority on boards and committees.

Also, they are the church's "squeaky wheels" who attract all the attention. Ellis writes, "They are a vocal minority and exert an influence far out of proportion to their numbers."[9] The typical church is led by pastors and boards who strive to please everyone. They are convinced that a function of their leadership is to keep all the people happy all the time, which is not possible. Consequently, those who oppose change discover that constant complaining translates into power, especially if they threaten to withhold their tithe or leave the church. To keep them happy, the pastors and boards give in to their demands. The result is that a noisy minority controls the quiet majority.

The change agent must understand from the start that the ministry of revitalization involves working with never adopters. This means several things. The first is that the never adopters will adamantly oppose their plans for change. If the potential leader of change has a difficult time emotionally with strong opposition, then he will need to repent or find another ministry. The second is that these people may never be won over. This means living with and attempting to minister to people for whom there is little or no hope of resolution. While some may stay around and function much like a perpetual splinter under the pastor's fingernail, eventually most will either storm out or quietly slip out the back door of the church. The third is that they can be very abrasive. They are usually angry, critical people, and the change agent becomes their primary object of ventilation. While he may wear thick skin, his family does not. This can be the deciding factor that births the leader's resignation.

Middle Adopters

The middle adopters are located between the two extremes—the early and never adopters. The middle adopters are clearly in the majority, for they make up 60 to 80 percent of the church. They are the key group because their response to the leader or the change agent will determine whether or not the church is revitalized.

Middle adopters, like never adopters, reflect all four temperaments on the *Personal Profile*. However, the majority are the high S's and C's who tend to vote for the status quo unless they are given a good reason for change or are assured that change will not result in a loss of quality. On the *Keirsey Temperament Sorter*, many are NF's.

They have much in common with the "man from Missouri," the "show-me" state, which for years had a reputation for being resistant to change. For visionary people, believing is seeing. They have the intuitive capacity to see things in their heads long before they become realities. However, for nonvisionary people (the man from Missouri), seeing is believing. They will not act until they have seen all the evidence.

104

These people are ambivalent toward change. More inclined toward the status quo, they do not actively pursue change nor will they automatically reject it. When confronted with new ideas and proposals, they prove to be cautious, skeptical, and full of questions. While the change agent views them as overly cautious, they prefer to be thought of as conservative.

Win Arn believes that the middle adopters are more easily influenced by those resistant to change than those who support it.[10] Therefore, the leader of change may feel some initial resistance. In general, however, they want to go along with the pastor and withhold a verdict until more of the evidence is in. They need time to adjust to any new ideas or proposals. Their tendency is to sit back and watch what happens. They have the potential for change but not today; maybe tomorrow. The change agent must make sure that tomorrow becomes today.

In the process of leading middle adopters through change, leaders need to maximize communication. They must clearly and carefully confront middle adopters with all of the facts behind their reasons for change. At the same time they need to pursue authenticity of information, because some middle adopters are carefully analyzing and evaluating all that is being said. They respond to inaccuracy and a seeming lack of integrity with deaf ears.

Late Adopters

The late adopters are found on the change-resistance continuum between the middle adopters and the never adopters. Win Arn writes that the late adopters represent as much as 18 percent of the congregation and sets the never adopters at 2 percent.[11]

Arn notes that the late adopters are the last in the church to endorse a new idea or program of change. Like the never adopters, they are often articulate and can be expected to speak out against anything new or innovative.[12] In general they are indistinguishable from the never adopters, which initially gives the impression that the never adopters are numerically larger than they are. The difference, however, is that in time the late adopters go along with the new idea or proposal. While they may never acknowledge it verbally, they will fall in line with the direction of the majority or middle adopters; as the majority goes, so go the late adopters. Again, this is why the middle adopters are so important to the ultimate revitalization of the church.

The problem with the late adopters is that they go along with change but are not necessarily convinced of the need for change. The fact that they reluctantly raise their hands in favor or quietly say yes at the final vote does not translate into changed hearts. It only means that they have resigned themselves to the fact that some change in the church is inevitable. Consequently, they may take the place of the recently departed never adopters as the church's guardians of the status quo and serve as its squeaky wheels.

Actually this is not all bad. Whether they realize it or not, they will serve to keep the change agent honest. They provide a certain degree of accountability. Since they will always be looking over his shoulder, he must be careful not to become sloppy in his thinking or arbitrarily introduce changes that are not in the best interests of the church. If he does, he can expect these church referees to throw down the flag and march off a stiff penalty.

Leith Anderson is the author of *Dying for Change* and the pastor of Wooddale Church in the Minneapolis suburb of Eden Prairie, Minnesota. Wooddale is a revitalized church that illustrates how important a recognition of the four categories of change is to the change agent. Anderson writes: "The whole procedure took months. The large majority agreed and accepted the changes; a few disagreed and left; others disagreed and stayed. The results were major in terms of redirection and significant changes."[13] Pastor Anderson and those who early initiated the new proposal represent the early adopters. The large majority who agreed and accepted the changes were the middle adopters. The few who disagreed and left were the never adopters. Others who disagreed and stayed were the late adopters.

Part 2: The Levels of Opinion Makers

In his book *Dying for Change*, Leith Anderson points out that most organizations have levels or layers of opinion makers who either formally or informally exert influence that can be used to accomplish change.[14] His advice to change agents is to identify and persuade these primary informal leaders of the organization, and they will convince everyone else. He writes, "And when they are convinced that change is needed, the battle is won."[15] Anderson ranks them in four concentric circles of increasing size (see figure 11).

Figure 11
Layers of Opinion Makers

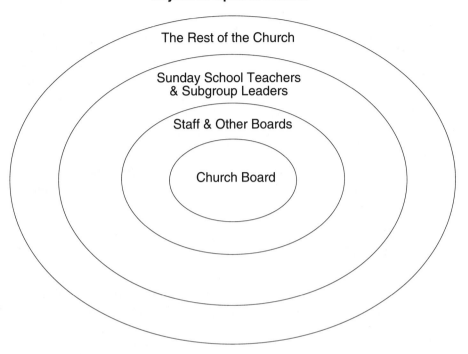

The Rest of the Church

Sunday School Teachers
& Subgroup Leaders

Staff & Other Boards

Church Board

The Members of the Church Board

The members of the church governing board are located at the center of the circle. Right or wrong, most long-established churches have a group of part-time voluntary lay leaders who sit on a board and serve the church primarily by making decisions about anything from the relocation of the facility to the color of the daffodils outside the nursery.[16]

The people on this board represent the formal leadership of the church and often make up the informal leadership as well. There may be only one or two or as many as twenty or thirty people, depending on the size of the church. Pastor Gary's church of seventy members has five including himself.

Assuming they are the primary opinion makers, any revitalization program begins with them. In describing the transformation that took place at Wooddale Church in the early 1980s, Anderson writes that initially "a few leaders developed an early vision of an

107

outreaching church."[17] Then, "after dozens of meetings and hundreds of hours of discussion, the rest of the board members were convinced."[18]

The wise leader should initiate the change process by determining where each board person is on the change-response continuum. Chances are excellent that they will be sprinkled through all four categories, the largest number being middle adopters. In an attempt to appear fair to the rest of the congregation (at least the "squeaky wheels"), most lay boards or lay-board nominating committees will proportion board membership according to the number of church members represented in each of the four change-response categories. A board of six people (not including the pastor) might typically consist of one early adopter, three middle adopters, one late adopter, and one never adopter. The rationale is that this approach fairly represents the various interest groups in the congregation who must feel they have a voice in the church's affairs.

The change agent, even before he accepts a call to the church, can use the board as a weather gauge to gain an early reading of how the winds of change are blowing in the congregation. There are several approaches. One is to ask individual board members innocent questions related to the potential for implementing change. A question might be, "Has anyone ever attempted to change the order of worship?" or, "How would the congregation respond if a guest speaker preached from a different version of the Bible?" The candidate should beware that some people will seem optimistic about change in conversations prior to his acceptance of a call, but show resistance after he assumes the position. Another approach is to call or correspond with the former pastor. Inquire as to why he left the church, and ask if he has any advice or words of wisdom for its next pastor, especially if he is a change agent. Ultimately, if the board consists of early adopters, then the pastor should be optimistic. If the same board is made up predominantly of never adopters, he politely responds to a call with "no thanks."

In the 1990s most boards reflect the makeup found above where there is a member or two on either fringe but most are middle adopters. There is great hope for boards with this configuration; they can change, but change is not automatic. The majority of boards are typically led by a key lay leader of influence who is called the chairman of the board. If this leader is an early adopter, the chances for change should receive an A or B grade. If he is a middle adopter, the grade is a B or C. If he is a late or never adopter, do not wait around for the report card.

The Staff and Members of Other Boards

Anderson writes, "The next to be convinced were also leaders— church staff and members of other boards."[19] If the leader of change determines that the majority of the lay board are open to or behind his taking the church in a new direction, then he is ready to approach any staff members and the other boards.

Actually, the new change agent should interact with any full- or part-time staff while consulting with the board. The staff people are a vital part of the team. If they are not supportive of the new vision, then they will need to be replaced. This possible option must be an item for discussion on a board level. The same principle applies in situations where the present pastor catches a new vision for the church that is not in accord with that of any of the existing staff. In an attempt to keep all the members happy all the time, most lay boards are reluctant to let any staff person go for any reason. They seldom see the wisdom in releasing those with another vision, and the results can prove disastrous.

Except in the smallest of churches there will be additional boards. These consist of the missions committee, the Christian education board, the building committee, and others. The change agent who overlooks these boards—especially their leadership— makes a fatal error in judgment. In light of their public positions and the fact that some are in elected places of leadership, they are, as someone has said, "a force to be reckoned with." Several even represent future church board members. Without their support, the ministry will fragment into various disparate pieces. Anderson cogently observes, "These people need a fair share of time to process the changes; it was not reasonable to expect them to accept in one hour what had taken others nearly one year. . . . As they processed the proposed changes, they asked some new questions and came up with some new ideas. Plans were revised and improved from their input."[20]

The Sunday School Teachers and Subgroup Leaders

Anderson writes, "The next circle of Wooddalers included Sunday school teachers and the leaders of growth groups, youth groups, choirs, and other subgroups in the church."[21] Perhaps more than any other people in the congregation, these teachers and leaders occupy positions of significant influence in the lives and opinions of others. It is these often-behind-the-scenes people who are "up to their elbows" in the actual ministries of the church and who form the very leadership backbone of the entire local body.

Ministries such as a Sunday school class, growth group, or youth group touch people's lives directly and intimately. The choir is a case in point. Over the years I have heard more pastors in traditional churches lament the fact that the members of the choir were either a blessing or a curse. While this sounds strong, many trace their biggest problems back to certain people in the choir who spread damaging misinformation. Consequently, the leaders of these ministries become vital links in the lines of communication from the pastor and board to each particular member and attender. They have the subtle power to promote new ideas or inflict significant damage on a ministry.

Regarding these people, Anderson writes, "Again it was necessary to take them through much of the initial process; and again there were some new questions and new ideas and a further refinement of the plans."[22]

The Rest of the Church

Anderson relates that in this last step the proposed changes were shared with the rest of the church. This recognizes that the first three levels, though very influential and critical to any change process, generally make up only 10 to 20 percent of the people in the church. The other 80 to 90 percent represent the rest of the members and attenders.

Some of these people, though not active in leadership, can be articulate voices for the status quo. They may insist on "coloring within the lines" and live in yesterday. If the church's polity is not congregational, others are likely to vote with their feet. And no one likes surprises. Therefore, at Wooddale the proposed changes were communicated through such events as open forums, home meetings, special presentations, and business meetings.[23]

What was the situation at Chapel Hill Community Church? Four men sat on the board of the church. One was an early adopter, two were middle adopters, and one was a never adopter. The one early adopter was largely frustrated because the never adopter strongly influenced the two middle adopters. Every time a new idea surfaced, the never adopter rehearsed all the reasons why it would not work. For the next six months the board dissected and discussed the issue until all the life went out of it. When they finally voted, the proposal was insipid and had lost its original punch.

The average pastor might see this as a losing proposition. Not Pastor Gary. He was excited. The situation presented a challenge. The door of change was slightly open and a ray of hope shined through. His presence would add another early adopter to the board. He believed that God could use the two of them to exert a strong influence on the two middle adopters to move the church in a new direction. The experience would not be without its difficult moments. There would be some harsh words, insinuations, and even some accusations. His character would be carefully scrutinized. But facing pain was a part of the job description for a change agent. He believed he knew what he was getting into.

7

The Times for Change
Windows that Open and Shut

Pastor Gary and his wife had driven to a suburb located not far from Chapel Hill Community Church to look for a house prior to moving into the community. Since they were so close, they decided to drop by the church. As they neared the facility, they noticed a thin wisp of smoke rising in the distance. The thought that the church might be on fire never crossed their minds until a fire truck rushed past them with siren wailing and turned in just ahead of them at the church.

There was a lot of excitement at Chapel Hill that day. A short in the electrical box located in a makeshift tool shop next to the sanctuary had gutted the room and spread smoke to other parts of the facility. The damage was not extensive but would require some remodeling and the painting of the sanctuary.

Before noon, a number of people in the congregation had heard the news and dropped by to learn the details. The responses varied. Several joked nervously, while others looked concerned. Some shed a few tears of joy that the entire facility had not been razed. Later, on the way back home when he had had sufficient time to collect his thoughts, Pastor Gary wondered why God let this happen. And why did it happen just before his arrival at the church? He believed that God is sovereign and in control of the affairs of men. Is there some way that this crisis along with his arrival at the church could be used to point the church in a new direction? His question had to do with the time of change. Are certain times bet-

113

ter for change than others? When might Pastor Gary introduce a new proposal at Chapel Hill Community Church?

Often people confuse the church with its building. According to Scripture, the church is people (Acts 8:1–3; 9:3), not a facility. And just as people have a life cycle, every church has a life cycle consisting of birth, growth, decline, and eventually death (figure 12). Win Arn writes, "Many churches begin a plateau and/or slow decline around their 15th–18th year. 80–85 percent of the churches in America are on the downside of this growth cycle."[1]

Arn observes, however, that there are certain times in the history of the typical church when its life cycle can be interrupted, when "interventions" present opportunities for the implementation of change. Arn writes: "Growth does not *necessarily* occur after an intervention, but the likelihood increases. In church growth terminology, it is a 'period of receptivity' for the church."[2]

The alert change agent views these interruptions or interventions in the church's life as open windows for potential change. The church's windows periodically open and close. The open windows remain open for only a short period of time before they close. While the change agent can open some of the windows, others God has to open. The skillful pastor must be alert to the various windows that are open and be ready to use them to accomplish biblical change before they close and the opportunity is lost. But what are some of these windows? What do they look like? How would a leader of change know one if he saw it?

A Widely Perceived Crisis

A crisis has the greatest potential to initiate change in the typical church. Scripture is replete with examples of how God raised up strong leaders of change to lead his people in a crisis. God used Joseph and the evil intentions of his brothers to save many lives in crisis (Gen. 50:19–20). God raised up Moses to lead Israel out of an intolerable situation in Egypt (Exod. 3:8). God touched the life of Nehemiah and used him in the lives of the Jews who had escaped the captivity in Jerusalem (Neh. 1:2–11).

However, as many people as possible must become aware of the crisis. If there is a crisis and no one recognizes it, then not much will happen. In Acts 6:1 the early church was not aware that it had a crisis until the Grecian Jews complained that their widows were being neglected. The situation is comparable to a person with a

114

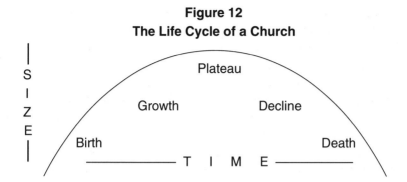

Figure 12
The Life Cycle of a Church

cancer that goes undetected until it is too late. People have to know something is seriously wrong so they will move to remedy the situation.

This is the major problem facing churches in the 1990s poised to enter the next millennium and many are not aware of it. Others suspect something might be wrong, but they are afraid to go to the doctor because he might confirm their worst fears.

A crisis can take many forms. One is when the senior citizens in the church far outnumber the younger. Eventually the congregation looks around and realizes that without a new generation of younger believers the church's days are numbered. One of the advantages of aging is that God takes his people home, and they experience no more suffering, mourning, or pain (Rev. 21:4). However, if these saints are not replaced, the church also faces certain death.

Another is a plateau or decline in attendance. Most churches do not view a plateau as a crisis. As long as they maintain the status quo then all must be well. However, a plateau is the precursor of a decline. When the decline arrives, it announces its presence through such events as a serious drop in income, a significant loss of manpower, or a facility that dwarfs the congregation. This captures people's attention and may catalyze a positive commitment toward change.

A third crisis is the resignation or retirement of the pastor. If he is a young person, then God mysteriously moves in his life, and he is called to another church, or he returns to the seminary to pursue doctoral studies. If he is near retirement, then God sends him visions of joining and ministering to a community of older people in Florida or Arizona.

115

A fourth is a natural disaster that damages or destroys the church facility. On Christmas day in 1975, fire destroyed the facility of historic Scofield Memorial Church in downtown Dallas, Texas. Prior to the fire, attendance had declined considerably, and most of the congregation were people in the later years of life. A number of former members had moved to the suburbs, and only a few continued to drive back downtown to attend church. The future looked grim. However, the congregation responded heroically to the crisis by making a number of decisions, the most difficult of which was to relocate to the suburbs of Dallas. God has blessed this decision, and attendance has now doubled through an influx of younger couples over the last few years.

Other crises are a church split, the moral lapse of a pastor or staff member, the firing of a pastor, a lawsuit, an aging, obsolete facility, and many others. The key is for leaders to develop "crisis-sensitive eyes." They must be quick to spot a potential crisis and use it to point the church in a new direction.

The power of a crisis to accomplish change is pain. Crises interrupt the status quo in an emotionally painful way. And pain has a way of gaining everyone's attention. No one enjoys pain, whether it is physical, emotional, or spiritual. Consequently, at the onset of a particular crisis, most people begin the quest for pain relief. The wise, loving leader of change faces the congregation with its pain and proposes God's viable solutions to remedy that pain.

A Change of Pastors

A pastoral change can motivate the revitalization of a congregation. God often uses this window-opening event to implement a new vision for the church. The advantage is that the church grants the new pastor a certain amount of leverage. The resignation or removal of the former pastor disrupts the congregational status quo. Next, people realize the new pastor is not aware of "how we do things around here." They also want to make a good first impression; they want the pastor to like them. Third, the board is relieved to have someone fill the pastoral office. They were not aware of how much the former pastor accomplished until he left. The result is an initial willingness to flex.

However, most advise new pastors not to attempt any substantial changes during the first year. For example, in 1962 Perry and Lias wrote, "Make no major changes during the first year on a

116

field."[3] Another writes, "The axiom proves true: Don't make major changes in the first two years of ministry; establish trust first."[4] Pastoral students hear the same advice from respected professors while in seminary or college. This is good advice for plateaued churches. However, recent evidence indicates that the honeymoon period may be the best time to introduce new ideas to the congregation.

In *Create Your Own Future!* Lyle Schaller writes concerning new pastors in declining churches:

> Experience suggests that (a) the greater the need for a redefinition of the role of that parish, and/or (b) the more competitive the local ecclesiastical scene, and/or (c) the longer that pattern of decline has prevailed, the more critical it is for a newly arrived pastor to focus on reversing that decline during the first several months of that new pastorate. If the reversal is not underway by the end of the first eighteen months of the pastorate, it probably will not happen without radical changes. This generalization is consistent with the tradition of taking advantage of that honeymoon first year in a new pastorate.[5]

Churches which are in decline and aware of it often respond favorably to significant change during the honeymoon with the new pastor. There is a sense that if we do not act now, there may be no tomorrow.

Robert Thomas lists three advantages for implementing change early in the new pastorate of a declining small church:

1. The pastor avoids the pitfall of becoming identified with the status quo.
2. A foundation can be laid on which to build momentum for future changes when resistance is likely to be greater.
3. The pastor is perceived as a change agent and hence the tendency is to expect him to continue introducing new, innovative ideas.[6]

The situation is different in plateaued churches. Concerning the small, plateaued church Schaller writes, "Planning to move up off a plateau in size, especially in congregations averaging fewer than 160 at worship, usually is extremely difficult."[7] Since about 95 percent of all churches in North America average one hundred people

117

or less at worship,[8] he is describing much of churched America. They are satisfied as long as they can pay the bills and experience little or no shortage in manpower. They are deceived by the status quo into thinking all is well. They are not aware that a plateau precipitates decline. When it strikes, they are caught unprepared.

There are some exceptions. Kirk Hadaway writes: "If lay leaders withhold permission in a small church, the pastor can do nothing, but if they grant even tacit approval, then it is possible for the pastor to tap into dormant purposes of the church, gain a few allies and begin the process of revitalization. Nowhere is this more evident than when a new minister comes to a small church which is willing to change."[9]

More often the new pastor in a plateaued church has to earn the right to lead the ministry through the change process. It may take some time to build necessary credibility with a plateaued congregation. Schaller indicates that the most effective time for leadership in the average pastorate is years five through eight.[10] Hadaway writes:

> In a survey of growing, plateaued, and declining Southern Baptist churches it was found that *growing* churches were more likely to have pastors with tenures of *four years or more* than were plateaued or declining churches. Conversely, *declining* churches were *much* more likely to have pastors with tenures of *under two years* than were plateaued or growing churches.[11]

At the same time the average pastoral tenure among Protestant denominations in the United States is 3.7 years.[12] Hadaway writes, "Survey results show that 25 percent of declining churches have had four or more pastors in the past decade, as compared to only 5 percent of growing churches."[13] Far too many pastors unknowingly vacate their churches prior to the years of their most effective ministry. We need a new generation of authentic leaders in Christ's church who are not quick to quit at the first sign of trouble but are willing to intentionally commit themselves to longer terms of ministry in service of the Savior.

As in the small church, exceptions do exist in large churches. However, the situation is different in larger plateaued churches. Hadaway indicates that a few larger churches will respond to the leadership of a honeymoon pastor because they have "pent up" growth waiting for the right leadership and motivation. He writes:

"As indicated earlier, survey data clearly shows that if churches are going to break off the plateau, they tend to do so very quickly (within the first two years of a pastorate) or else it takes much longer (after at least five years). There are almost no examples where breakout growth began during years three through five of a pastor's tenure."[14]

A Renewal of the Pastor

In *Your Church Can Grow*, Pete Wagner writes, "In America, the primary catalytic factor for growth in a local church is the pastor."[15] As the pastor of the church goes, so goes the church, or perhaps a better expression: As the pastor of the church grows, so grows the church. The problem is that many pastors in plateaued or declining churches become discouraged and drop out. They often take another more promising church. Some return to seminary for doctoral studies. An alarming number drop out of the ministry entirely. A better alternative is to pursue and experience pastoral renewal.

A number of exciting, high-impact ministries across North America are accomplishing significant ministries for the Savior. Often these churches conduct pastors' conferences in which they share various biblical and practical principles that have enhanced their ministries. Two examples are Saddleback Valley Community Church, located south of Los Angeles, and Willow Creek Community Church, located west of Chicago. Numerous pastors have attended these two excellent conferences and experienced emotional and spiritual revival of their spirits. They discover that not only is God still blessing churches in the twentieth century but that he can bless their ministries as well. In particular, pastors give testimony of how the authentic spirituality of leaders such as Bill Hybels and Rick Warren have refreshed their own spirits and encouraged them in their personal recommitment to God.

In addition, several organizations conduct seminars or provide video and audio tapes and other materials for pastors who desire to learn more about various aspects of ministry such as church planting, church renewal, principles of leadership, and so on. One example is the Charles E. Fuller Institute of Evangelism and Church Growth located in Pasadena, California. Another is Church Growth, Inc., located in Monrovia, California.

Gradually leaders who have encountered significant problems and discovered some vital answers are writing books that can be most helpful to the pastor in a plateaued or declining situation. They have designed their books to provide both information and encouragement. The information consists of biblical and practical principles which have been applied to struggling churches with encouraging results. The encouragement often comes from biblical and contemporary ministry examples. Again, they communicate the truth that God cares about his church and desires to see people turn to him in the midst of difficult times.

Every pastor struggles with discouragement at some point in his ministry. If it happened to Paul (2 Tim. 4:9–18), it will happen to the best of pastors. Therefore, wise pastors take advantage of the opportunity to attend a pastors' conference or a seminar every year, or at the least every two years, and regularly read books that provide helpful insight and encouragement.

The Planting of a Church

Not only should churches birth other churches, but one means of encouraging change in established churches is the open window of church planting. Gary Carter, pastor of Eastwood Fellowship Baptist Church in Saint Thomas, Ontario, points out that there are times when churches need to experience a pruning process. The benefits of pruning a church are similar to that of pruning a tree. He writes:

> We all know there is more growth work to be done in our own churches. But even a novice gardener also knows that at times you encourage a tree by pruning it. The secret is deciding when and how to prune productively. If we don't prune our churches for growth at the proper time, one of two things is bound to happen: (1) stagnation will set in, or (2) accidental pruning will occur. Accidental pruning is a group splitting off or people simply "dying on the vine."[16]

Then Pastor Carter compares the benefits of birthing new churches to the productive pruning of a tree:

> Thus, when a church has not seen recent growth, it may be a signal that it is time to prune—by planting a daughter church. Such a move is likely to stimulate the church to new heights by breaking

in on the established relationships and patterns in a positive way. Growth will be spurred again by the recent memories of how the sanctuary used to be full. Everyone will know that these pews are now empty because the church selflessly gave people to the daughter church. A holy dissatisfaction will engender enthusiasm to fill those places once again. The new-found momentum may take the mother church to the next plateau that previously seemed out of reach.[17]

Church birthing may provide the solution for numerous established churches that cling to the status quo while they experience a generational clash. As the baby boom generation grows into their forties, they are moving into positions of power and influence on their church boards. At the same time they are pushing for significant changes. One example is the church's worship; they want more contemporary music. However, the older preboomer generation strongly resists these changes, opting for traditional worship and the good old hymns of the past. The result is often disastrous. Either the church splits or one generation walks out and leaves the church and its responsibilities to the other.

In this situation it would make better sense to plant a church. Rather than split or empty the change-resistant traditional church, why not use it and its resources to plant a church for the boomers where they can worship with a more appropriate style? Thus both generations win. The mother church is challenged to grow and will experience some change and revitalization simply by going through the birth process. The new church will grow and reach a new generation for the Savior.

Church planting is an exciting option for dying churches. Some congregations are beginning to view their death as an opportunity to give life. One congregation disbanded several years ago and entrusted their property to Interest Ministries, who sold the building to a new Hispanic congregation at a greatly reduced price. Income from the sale was used for the retirement of three missionaries from the former church and for other church planting work.[18] A Baptist church in Dallas had declined to around thirty members. The future looked grim. Consequently, the congregation decided to sell the facility and pour the resources into a church plant in a nearby growing community. Some of the congregation joined the planted church, while others disbursed into various churches in the community. Approximately two years later the growing church plant anticipates at least two hundred to three hundred people in worship each Sunday and is renting a sizable space in a strip mall.

A Renewal of the Lay Leadership

An overlooked window of change is a renewal of the church's board of leaders. Not only pastors can experience renewal; lay leaders may go through the same experience. Arn writes, "If the church's mission is clearly rediscovered by lay leadership, it can provide an intervention event and possible change."[19]

The lay board in churches may be resistant to change for different reasons. One is the makeup of the board in terms of change response. If a majority of the board consists of late adopters or never adopters, not much change will occur. Another is that some boards have grown accustomed to the status quo. It is a lot easier in some ways to maintain a church than to risk change. While the "squeaky wheels" and others may still complain, at least they do not walk out and take their tithes with them.

A third reason a board may reject change is because they do not grasp the change agent's vision for the ministry. They may be open to change but refuse to act until they have a clearer picture of the new direction. In some instances the church has never had a vision. In others the vision is changing. In these situations wise leaders will involve their boards in renewal. There are several ways to accomplish lay renewal. One is to educate the board as much as possible in biblical principles of change and renewal. Together they could read current books on leadership or the spiritual life.[20] They might study change from the perspective of Nehemiah or some other change agent of the Bible.

Another alternative is to attend a visionary, cutting-edge church conference or seminar. Andy McQuitty is the pastor of Irving Bible Church located northwest of Dallas, Texas. He took his board to hear Rick Warren at a conference center in the mountains of scenic Colorado. This conference heavily influenced the men toward a new vision for the church. Consequently, while Andy cast a new vision for Irving Bible Church, he also used Rick Warren to aid him in the process.

A third is to ask your leaders to listen to or view audio and video cassette tapes from new-paradigm churches that God is blessing. These cassettes can accomplish a number of purposes such as the articulation of a vision, the communication of new worship formats, and so on. Before introducing any change to the governing board, ask each leader individually to listen to a visionary sermon on an audio tape or view a video of a more contemporary church service. After a week, meet with that person informally over lunch and ask what he thinks. Be sure to answer any questions and clear up any misconceptions. Ask the leader if he would favor the move in a new direction. Most often this approach catalyzes new vision and ignites innovation among the church's leaders.

Randy Frasee, pastor of Pantego Bible Church in Arlington, Texas, has worked through the revitalization process with his board of elders. The men are at a point in their development where they regularly read books and listen to tapes so that they can keep this exciting church on the cutting edge of ministry in America.

The Expertise of a Church Consultant

Often churches do not value or have confidence in the leadership of the pastor for a multitude of reasons both good and bad. A young pastor may have to be patient in winning the confidence of the church's senior members. Those who are highly educated may not value the leadership of a pastor who lacks a college or seminary education. People with lots of experience in their professions may question the capabilities of a pastor with little experience in the ministry. Members with strong leadership abilities in the marketplace struggle with pastors who have limited leadership capabilities. Those who have weathered personal difficulties with the former leader may be slow to respond to a new pastor.

In any situation where the pastor does not have the allegiance of the board and/or the congregation, a church consultant can serve effectively. Qualified, skilled consultants bring a certain objectivity to a situation that instills confidence. They can spot problems and suggest solutions that often translate into change.

Some pastors may have the people's confidence in their leadership knowledge and abilities. However, they may find themselves in a situation where they need the wisdom and advice of a specialist such as a consultant. This applies to a building program, church planting, church revitalization, a ministry to the handicapped, and others.

Churches without pastors would be wise to seek the advice of a consultant before pursuing any new ventures. Lay people tend to view the ministry differently than a business. Many are convinced that they know as much about leadership and the ministry as a pastor. (And in certain situations they do. Some seminary graduates are well prepared to study and teach the Bible but know virtually nothing about leadership and the practical aspects of a ministry.) The result is that these earnest laymen make numerous mistakes that deeply affect the ministry. A consultant can provide them with the expertise to facilitate the ministries of the church and influence them to make critical changes.

Denominational Assistance

Some denominations are in a position to offer assistance and direction to their churches. This may range from occasional pastoral advice to long-term professional consultation. People in these positions can provide an open window of change for the churches they work with. However, leaders of churches in some denominations complain that advisers and consultants are out to preserve the denominational status quo and are death to change.

Other Windows

Win Arn suggests several other open windows for change. One is a revival. Some churches and denominations believe that revivals accomplish renewal and change. Arn seriously questions their ability to intervene in the life of most churches in the 1990s.[21] They worked well for the churched preboomer generation but appear to have lost their effectiveness with the baby boom and baby bust generations.

A second is a church-wide growth seminar. Arn sees its value in serving as a spark to ignite new growth. Large numbers of people may attend these seminars and are exposed to and discuss the various intervention events mentioned in this chapter as well as other new paradigm concepts.[22]

Another is to close the church. This involves pronouncing the last rites for a dying church. In effect it accelerates the inevitable. Then after six to nine months, a new or renewed pastor starts over with a new group of people and/or those in the old church who have the same vision.[23] The new church has several options. First, it may plant, using the same location and the old facilities. Second, the new church could sell the old property and facilities and use the funds to jump start a new work in another community. Third,

124

the new group could plant two churches, one in the old facilities and another in a different community in the area. Whichever option the leader follows, new life is born out of certain death.

Wise pastors who desire to lead their churches through the change process are constantly sensitive to the various windows of opportunity; they develop "opportunity eyes." These leaders can open some windows at their own initiative, such as the use of a consultant, the planting of a church, and renewal. Other windows such as a crisis or a revival are initiated by God. As these open, change agents are quick to spot them and use them to cast a new vision for their ministries. When several windows open at the same time, they realize the chances for change increase proportionately.

Win Arn offers the following warning to change agents with "opportunity eyes":

> *An intervention event, by itself, will not produce growth* . . . the new pastor arrives and business continues; the sanctuary is rebuilt, the renewed pastor or lay leader loses enthusiasm or leaves; the seminar is forgotten. Intervention events only create "windows of opportunity" which, for a limited time, create an environment where growth is *more likely* to occur—*if appropriate strategy is applied.*[24]

The leader of change must be proactive; he must act while the window is open. He must understand the process of change and be ready to implement that process as God opens windows to the future. But what is the process of change? What does it look like? The process of change is the topic of the next chapter.

8

The Process of Change
How to Change

In evaluating the various short-term ministries of the men who had come to Chapel Hill Community Church since the founder, Pastor Gary observed that most were not change agents nor did they know very much about change. Since Chapel Hill could not support them, they had worked part-time: one was a mailman, one was an employee in a bank, and another was a seminary student. Consequently, their ministries were custodial. They functioned as caretakers and maintenance men who spent the bulk of their time caring for people and maintaining the status quo. Hoping for change, however, does not make things change. And when things do not change, discouragement quickly sets in. Most pastors have a low tolerance for discouragement. Once it gets into their bloodstream, it spreads quickly, and they are gone. Such was the pastoral history at Chapel Hill.

Pastor Gary refused to make the same mistakes. He was a change agent, not a maintenance man. The term *custodian* could not be found on his resumé, and he would not function as a ministry fireman putting out ministry fires. If Chapel Hill Community Church could shake free from its cobwebs and pursue a new direction, he was the man for the job. However, his approach was not to hope for change. Change agents make things change by being catalysts of the process. The question is, How? What is the change process?

Before Pastor Gary climbs into the overalls of a farmer and attempts to plant the seeds of change in his congregational garden, he must first prepare the soil for change. Preparation precedes the process and consists of three parts. The first is prayer. In John 15:5 the Savior warns, "Apart from me you can do nothing." Jesus Christ is the essential one who changes and builds churches (Matt. 16:18). Therefore, the leader of change must bathe the entire ministry in prayer. John Bunyan once said, "You can do more than pray once you've prayed, but you cannot do more than pray until you have prayed." However, prayer not only precedes the process, it permeates the process. The change agent will spend much time on his knees throughout the change process.

The second part of the process is evaluation. Pastor Gary and other change agents need to evaluate their congregations and determine if their churches are plateaued or in decline. This evaluation will help them decide how fast they move their churches through the process of change. As determined in the last chapter, the general principle is that a new pastor in a declining church will move quickly. As Schaller points out there are several variables such as how long the church has been in decline, the competitive nature of the local church scene, and the need to redefine the role of the church in the community. Size may also be a factor.[1] The generalization is that the pioneer pastor takes advantage of the leverage he has during the honeymoon to initiate the change process. If something does not happen soon to reverse the downward spiral, then *later* may become *never*.

However, if the new pastor comes into a plateaued church, then the general rule is to move more slowly unless the church understands its precarious position and had hired him to move it off the plateau. Pastor Rick Warren at Saddleback Valley Community Church advises: "Be patient. The longer a church has been at a plateau, the longer it takes to turn it around."[2]

The third part of the process is leadership. Is the new pastor the right man for the job? The belief of many who anticipate and prepare for professional ministry is, "I can do anything I want. If I want to be a pastor, then I can be a pastor." This clearly violates Paul's teaching in 1 Corinthians 12 and Romans 12; a hand cannot be a foot. The principle is that *who* is as important as *how*. Pastoring a church regardless of the situation is not for timid spirits. The pioneer who leads a church in a different, new direction must lead boldly and be prepared to pay a price. The wrong man in the wrong position leads to ministry burnout and, ultimately, ministry dropout.

Once the congregational soil is prepared for transition, the change agent is ready to plant the seeds of change. Studies of the methods of change find that the simplest and most influential is the method of Kurt Lewin. Lewin's formula, penned in 1943, has stood the test of time and much expansion and addition. The formula contains three steps:

1. Unfreeze the present situation.
2. Move to a new level.
3. Refreeze at the new level.[3]

In his book *The Mind Changers,* Em Griffin draws a helpful analogy between the change process in persuasion and making a candle. Persuasion that brings change consists of three steps: melt, mold, and make hard. To make a candle, first melt the wax, which corresponds to Lewin's unfreezing the present situation. Next, mold the soft wax into the shape of a candle, much as the change catalyst moves people to a new level. Finally, make the candle hard by allowing it to cool and resolidify. In the same way, the leader "makes hard" the change by refreezing it at a new level.[4]

Unfreeze the Present Situation

Frozen in the Status Quo

The leader of change initiates the transition process by unfreezing the church's present situation, especially in churches that cling to the status quo for whatever reasons. If these communities are to move in a new, significant direction, they must become discontent with "what is." This means that the leader creates discontent with the status quo. Lyle Schaller writes: "In any discussion of intentional change it is almost impossible to overstate the importance of discontent. Without discontent with the present situation there can be no planned, internally motivated and directed intentional change."[5] And this is the job of the change agent: to "rub raw the sores of discontent."[6]

Thawing Out the Status Quo

But how does this take place? How does the change agent "rub raw the sores of discontent"? There are two ways. The first is that God creates significant dissatisfaction with the status quo. He accomplishes this through such events as sickness, natural disasters, and various trials and tribulations. In the Old Testament Hezekiah became terminally ill, a large fish swallowed Jonah, the land of Palestine experienced periodic droughts, and Babylon constantly disrupted life in Israel. In the New Testament Paul suffered a thorn in the flesh, and God used persecution to spread the early church in Acts to Judea and Samaria. In addition, today God uses the "windows" described in chapter 7: a widely perceived crisis, a change of pastors, a renewal of the pastor, the planting of a church, a renewal of the lay leadership, the counsel of a church consultant, denominational assistance, a revival, a growth seminar, the closing of the church, and so on. Some personal events cause extreme stress such as death, sickness, a jail term, separation, divorce, marriage, and so on. God uses all these events to grab people by the lapels, get their attention, and shake them out of their lethargy.

God also uses change agents to initiate intentional discontent with "what is." He accomplishes this in a number of ways, all of which rest on the solid foundation of truth. In John 8:32 the Savior says, "Then you will know the truth, and the truth will set you free." Whatever form it takes, God's truth has a liberating effect. One means to create discontent is to point out the reality of the current situation. If some people cling to the status quo because they view reality as it "ought to be" or they are looking the other way, the agent of change is required to "tell it like it really is." A way to accomplish this is to expose the people to the information in chapter 2, "Dying for Change." The average churched person is not aware of these things. When people hear this information, they make the association between the typical American church and their church and become very uncomfortable. This approach is similar to but milder than Nathan's handling of David's sin against Uriah in 2 Samuel 11. In 2 Samuel 12, Nathan tells the story of how a rich man abused a poor man to stir David's anger. Then Nathan reveals that the story is an analogy and David is the rich man (2 Sam. 12:1–7).

Another more direct means of creating discontent is to use the information from chapter 2 to warn of an impending crisis. God's prophets in the Old Testament, such as Hosea, Amos, Obadiah, Micah, and others, used a similar technique. The change agent paints an ominous, candid picture of the future of the church if it does not change and make the necessary corrections now. He accomplishes this by giving the people the facts such as the church's average worship attendance, membership, and evangelism efforts over the last five, ten, or fifteen years. Any or all of these are plotted on the church's life cycle (figure 12 in chapter 7). Next, using this data, the change agent helps the people to project the church's future in its life cycle and asks, "Is this where you want to be five, ten, fifteen years from now?" Finally, he encourages everyone to become involved and rally to turn things around while there is still time. He preaches the reality that "if together we work hard, we can fend off the crisis and make a difference in our community for Christ." While ineffective leaders typically downplay the crisis, the effective leader uses the notion of impending disaster to motivate the church to engage the crisis and move toward change.

A third means of creating discontent is to call attention to the church's image in the community. Nehemiah calls attention to the poor image of the Jews in Jerusalem when he says, "Come, let us rebuild the wall of Jerusalem, and we will no longer be in disgrace." His point is that if the people will respond to his vision, they can correct their disastrous image in the Jerusalem community. When a church plateaus, and particularly when it declines, people in the community are aware of what is happening. Churches, like people, develop a reputation, and plateaued and declining churches develop a negative reputation in their individual communities. Both churched and unchurched people in the area may view that church as a battleground for feuding saints or as the run-down facility that is adversely affecting the values of their homes. Wise pastors, like Nehemiah, call attention to the poor reputation and exhort the people to work hard at changing that image.

A fourth means is to remind people of the church's "better days." This calls attention to the fact that something is terribly wrong with the status quo; things are not what they used to be. The people have either forgotten or strayed from their former values, which God blessed in the past. The wise leader will use the nostalgia and the difficult circumstances as a foundation to build a better tomorrow. It can serve as a rallying point to encourage people to value evangelism and serve one another in Christ. The pastor calls for a return not to the "good old days" (Phil. 3:13–14) but to the biblical values that made the old days good.

131

A fifth means of creating dissatisfaction with the present is to proclaim the church's best interests and desires and show how the status quo works contrary to those interests. For example, people value their church and desire that it live a long, healthy life. However, they must realize that the status quo eventually ends in certain death. When America was a churched culture, older churches might decline to around twenty or thirty people but would plateau and remain at that size indefinitely. Today most declining churches are not able to apply the brakes and are painfully running off the end of the tracks. The cultural gap and the rate of change is so great that older, typical churches are being swept under. The congregation needs to know this.

A sixth means is to present change and innovation as opportunities rather than threats. The typical status quo congregation views change as a threat. Pastors as leaders should make every effort to communicate the positive advantages of change and how it will benefit the people in the church. There are always two sides to every innovation. The stagnant congregation first looks at the negative side. The leader must force them to turn the innovation over and look at the positive side as well. Then he must regularly remind them of its benefits. Caleb and Joshua were change agents who used this technique in Numbers 14:7–8 to remind complaining Israel that the land was exceedingly good and positive proof that the envisioned promised land was flowing with milk and honey. While some today view growth as the enemy of congregational intimacy, leaders must remind them of the benefits of assimilating new people into the church who provide a new source of friendships, help to bear the burdensome costs of operating and maintaining the church, and many others.

A seventh means is to challenge the congregation to become the best they can be. Since there are no perfect churches, each person in the church is discontented about something they may or may not have verbalized. The wise change agent will ask people both privately and publicly to identify all the things in the church that really annoy them. He will collect them and at the appropriate time (a congregational meeting, a sermon, and so on) use them to create a significant feeling of discontent. He could begin by quoting the old cliché: "If it ain't broke, don't fix it." Next he could remind everyone that as long as there are no perfect churches, there is something "broke" in every congregation. Then he could cover some of the things that, according to the people, are in need of repair. This would be followed by a challenge to work hard at becoming the best church possible.

As leaders of change seek to unfreeze the present situation, they must realize that they have a proactive role in the process. They, themselves, are catalysts as they implement the methods above and others. At the same time, they are not alone in their efforts. God works directly in the lives of the congregation as well to bring stress and added discomfort with the way things are. He, too, is "rubbing raw the sores of discontent." The combination of God's direct intervention and his work through the change agent makes unfreezing the status quo a highly probable event.

Move to a New Level

Once the present situation is sufficiently thawed, the next step is to move the congregation to a new level. This movement consists of three phases: cast a vision, develop a plan, and recruit a team.

Cast a Vision

Not only must a congregation become famished over *what is*, they must crave *what could be*. Disrupting the congregational status quo by itself is not enough to implement change. The wound is sore and raw and in need of healing. The key to implementing intentional congregational change is to cast or recast a powerful, significant vision. People in the church see what is, but do they see what could be—the exciting possibilities of the future? This becomes the responsibility of the visionary leader of change.

A vision for ministry exists on both a personal and an organizational level. Personal vision concerns the ministry vision of an individual in the church and is based on his or her unique, divine design. Organizational vision relates directly to the ministry of the church as a whole.[7]

An organizational ministry vision is a must. No church will survive in the decade of the 1990s or the twenty-first century without a single, focused vision. To attempt ministry without a significant, well-articulated vision is to invite ministry disaster. The primary reason is that a vision provides a ministry with direction. It answers the questions, Where is this church going? What will it look like two, five, or ten years from now? The church without a clear vision is going nowhere. Few would climb on board a cruise ship if the captain had no idea where he was going. How is the church any different? A vision is also critical to other factors such as the church's unity, motivation, finances, and evaluation.[8]

I define an organizational vision as a clear and challenging picture of the future of a ministry as its leadership believes it can and must be.[9] This definition has six key ingredients. First, the church's vision must be clear, for people cannot be expected to act on information they either do not have or cannot understand. They cannot focus on fog. Second, the vision must challenge the congregation to action. If people are not challenged by the vision, there really is no vision, and the vision statement is merely so much black printer's ink on a sterile piece of white paper. Third, a vision forms a mental picture. Vision is seeing the picture in the mind of the visionary leader. It is a snapshot of what the church will look like tomorrow or in the years to come. Fourth, the church's vision is always cast in terms of the future. It is a prophetic mental picture of what tomorrow looks like. It provides a glimpse into the ministry's future and its exciting possibilities. Fifth, a significant vision has great potential. It is highly feasible because it rests firmly on the bedrock of reality. The visionary is acutely aware that God is about to accomplish something special and wants to be a part of the process. Finally, the organizational vision must be compelling. It grabs hold of people and will not let go. They are convinced not only that it *can be* but that it *must be*. Many pastors find it difficult to sleep at night until the church is moving in the direction of the new dream.

As the paradigms for the church prior to the 1950s continue to self-destruct and collapse, God is raising up new paradigms of ministry as we approach the third millennium. Not only will churches minister in new and refreshing ways but so will their pastors. One critical function for new-paradigm pastors and leaders is the cultivation, communication, and constant clarification of the church's vision. As vision cultivators, they intuitively initiate and develop the church's unique ministry vision. Next, they serve as the primary communicators of that vision. Finally, they clarify the vision by constant evaluation and refocusing of the dream. Studies indicate that most people can remember the dream for about one month. Therefore, only as visionary change agents cast and recast the vision will people move to a higher level in the change process.

This was true of Nehemiah as God's change agent. Critical to the revitalization of the Jews in Jerusalem was his recasting of God's vision. These Jews, though in "great distress and reproach" (Neh. 1:2–3), had apparently grown used to the status quo. Nehemiah was deeply touched by their plight (Neh. 1:4) for his heart was grieved, and he wept and mourned for days. Jerusalem was the place where God had chosen his name to dwell (Neh. 1:9), yet it lay in a disastrous situation. Nehemiah could not tolerate this status quo. What kind of testimony was this to Israel's God? He could not rest until the situation was remedied. In Nehemiah 2:17 he calls the people's attention to the reality of their situation and casts the vision with the words: "Come let us rebuild the wall of Jerusalem."

There are several practical methods for articulating the dream. The first is the visionary's life. The leader's personal commitment to the vision communicates the vision by modeling the message. The second is the visionary's message. The message, which most often takes the form of a sermon or speech, communicates the vision. The third is the visual image. Visual images when explained remind people of the ministry's vision. Several examples of good visual images are a slide-tape presentation, a well-designed logo, a lapel pin, a tapestry, and others. The fourth is the church's programs. The ministries that actually take place in the church communicate the vision of the church regardless of what the church says in its official vision statement; what you see is what you get. Another is skits and drama. This art form is playing an increasingly important role in contemporary evangelical churches of the late twentieth century and will continue to do so in the twenty-first century. It is tailor made for vision casting. Other ways to communicate the vision are the newcomer's class, a year-end state-of-the-ministry sermon, a well-designed brochure, a special song, audio and video tapes, and so on.[10] The key to articulating the vision is not to pick and choose one of these methods but to use as many of them as possible. Since people can remember a vision for about one month, the church must regularly "parade" its dream by its people. The rule is: Repeat it over and over every day in a different way.

Develop a Plan

As the visionary leader of change intuitively initiates and develops the church's unique vision, he must develop an initial plan to implement that vision in the church. Kirk Hadaway notes that passive congregations normally expect their new pastors to arrive with a plan and a program.[11] The new pastor should not disappoint them.

In *The Leadership Challenge*, Kouzes and Posner emphasize the importance of planning to good leadership. They write:

> But it would be misleading to say that people will commit themselves to a course of action that is unconscious and unarticulated. High performance projects are carefully planned. No mountain climber would ever think of just setting out to scale a summit without selecting a route, choosing a competent team, assembling proper food and equipment, and so on. Every personal best we examined was characterized by attention to the details of planning and preparation.[12]

In *Say No, Say Yes to Change*, Dickson develops a formula for change. The formula looks like this:

$$A + B + C > D = CHANGE$$

The A represents a significant dissatisfaction with the status quo, and the B represents an awareness of an alternative better condition. The C represents "a knowledge of the first step(s) to take in changing to the better condition." D represents the costs of making the change, such as time, money, and physical and emotional energy. When significant dissatisfaction with the status quo, an awareness of a better condition, and a knowledge of the first steps for change overcome the costs of making change, then change occurs.[13] Dickson acknowledges the need to unfreeze the status quo and move the organization to a higher level through creating an awareness of a better alternative. But if people do not understand how to implement a plan to achieve the better alternative, it will not become a reality.

However, she uses the words *first steps* and not *a plan*. The reason is because the change agent often comes into the ministry from the outside and does not have enough information to attempt to implement a fully developed plan.

Thomas experienced this and writes:

> In order to address the burden, this writer responded to the call of a small, passive *status quo* congregation in southern California. This

means that the congregation had not increased by more than 10 percent in the three previous years. The approach was not to sit and observe 365 sunsets prior to acting. A theoretical plan of what needed to be done to revitalize the congregation was determined before this writer's arrival. Goals for the first two years were determined and objectives set so that progress could be measured. The implementation began immediately upon arrival.[14]

Thomas describes his plan as theoretical, consisting of goals and objectives for two years. Once the visionary leader is located in the new church, reality has a way of settling in quickly. If he has done his homework, some of his goals and objectives will be on target and will significantly impact the congregation. Thomas's church doubled in size and increased income 34 percent in the first year.[15] The leader will also discover realities and needs that he could not have been aware of while on the outside. This will force regular reassessments of the revitalization plan and whatever adjustments are necessary to reflect the reality of the actual congregational situation. The leader of change should not be surprised nor view this as negative. It is part and parcel of good short-range planning.

What kind of theoretical plan should the new pastor implement? What does a typical plan for change look like?[16] Obviously the answer depends on the individual congregation. Thorough, comprehensive plans include a mission statement derived from the vision statement, an evaluation of the church's current situation (needs, ministries, facilities, the demographics of the community, and so on), a statement of goals and/or objectives, the assignment of responsibilities to certain individuals, an action plan, a projected time of completion, an estimate of the costs (budget), and a review system to monitor progress. The initial plan should be concise and simple. Thomas's plan is seen in the following changes accomplished in the first year:

1. The establishment of a new vision.
2. The rewriting of the constitution's bylaws and mission's policy.
3. The remodeling of the sanctuary, kitchen, and bathrooms.
4. The change of the morning worship service to a more contemporary style.
5. The addition of 1,960 square feet of classroom space.
6. The addition of several new people-oriented programs.[17]

These changes reflect a plan primarily focused on people, programs, and physical plant. The establishment of a new vision and the addition of new people-oriented programs target *people*. The change of the style of worship and the addition of new programs focus on *program*. The remodeling of parts of the facility and the addition of classroom space affect the *plant*.

After arriving on the scene and reassessing his plan, Thomas reversed the above order to physical plant, program, and people. He discovered that the facilities were in such bad shape that new people would not be attracted to the church.[18] Also, some in the church are aware of unattractive facilities and some are not. Those who are see the church through visitor's eyes and are too embarrassed to invite outsiders. Those who are not see the facilities through rose-colored glasses. Over the years they have grown accustomed to the status quo.

Improving the facilities has several impacts on a church. First, outsiders who may be looking for excuses not to attend can find none. Second, it enhances congregational esteem. People gain a sense of accomplishment and begin to feel good about where they meet. They are cautious but ready for more change. A third factor is that repairing the physical plant is a quick, "small-win" process. Walls can be painted. Broken windows can be replaced. Grass can be mowed. At Irving Bible Church, located near Dallas, Texas, the first "small win" was a new church sign. Pastor Andy McQuitty says, "Suddenly, we had identity!" People view these goals as attainable in a short period of time, and then they can see the results. It instills pride in a good sense. This approach encourages the congregation to take the first step; it overcomes initial inertia. It is a quick victory that can be followed up with other quick "small wins."

Recruit a Team

In addition to cultivating and casting a vision and developing a plan, the change agent wears the hat of a recruiter. A key element in congregational revitalization is the recruitment of a vocal, articulate, visionary team to aid in the implementation of the dream. Hadaway writes:

> When things start moving, more and more members may become
> excited about the possibilities and begin to actively work toward the

dream. Throughout this process, continual effort must be made to develop allies among the existing lay leadership of the church and to create *new leaders* among those who are most excited about the vision. The goal is unity or "oneness of purpose" around a vision for what members hope the church will become.[19]

New Testament ministry is team ministry. The Savior chose not to act alone but through a team of disciples. Paul worked in tandem with numerous teams as modeled throughout the Book of Acts. It would prove unwise to think that leaders in the twenty-first century are an exception.

In most smaller churches this team includes a part-time, voluntary group of laymen who in most cases know very little about leadership and ministry in the church. As discussed in an earlier chapter, the leader of change needs to determine whether these individuals are early adopters, middle adopters, late adopters, or never adopters. The early adopters will be quick to join the team. The pastor should do everything possible throughout his tenure at the church to make them "heroes" before the membership. The congregation needs to esteem them. Next, with the help of the early adopters, the change agent will seek to win the middle adopters, who often make up the largest group on the board. Without these leaders on the team, change is not likely to happen.

Hadaway notes the importance of enlisting new leaders who have caught the vision. They will consist of other early adopters in the church community who are primed for change and have been patiently waiting for a catalyst to come along and ignite the process. Others are those who have come to the church after the new pastor and are younger than he. The pastor is wise to move those who are qualified into positions of leadership wherever possible in the church community. He could pursue the addition of one or two established, respected early adopters on the board. The others should be used as leaders in other critical positions in the community. They could replace late and never adopters who resign, or they could lead newly created ministries.

Refreeze at the New Level

Once the new changes are implemented, the ever-present temptation to slip back to the *way things were* will dog the leader's footsteps. This problem is not new, nor is it characteristic of the twentieth century only. In Numbers 14:1–3, Moses records the words of those who, though involved deeply in the change process, preferred the status quo of Egypt:

> That night all the people of the community raised their voices and wept aloud. All the Israelites grumbled against Moses and Aaron, and the whole assembly said to them, "If only we had died in Egypt! Or in this desert! Why is the LORD bringing us to this land only to let us fall by the sword? Our wives and children will be taken as plunder. Wouldn't it be better for us to go back to Egypt?" And they said to each other, "We should choose a leader and go back to Egypt."

Certain people will exert tremendous pressure to return to the "good old days" of the status quo. When something goes wrong, expect to hear the words "I told you so!" echo through the church. This is the second law of thermodynamics. One pastor compares it to a stretched rubber band pulling back to its original shape.[20] To preserve the progress and maintain momentum, the pastor must refreeze the changes and innovations at the new level.

The question is, How? The answer is found in Numbers 14. When Israel turned hostile to Moses and Aaron's transitional leadership, the two remained resistant—they hung tough. First, two early adopters, Caleb and Joshua, pointed to all the advantages of the new vision: "The land we passed through and explored is exceedingly good. If the LORD is pleased with us, he will lead us into that land, a land flowing with milk and honey, and will give it to us" (Num. 14:7–8). In effect, they said, "Can't you see how far we've come and what's just around the corner?" Next, they identified the real issues—rebellion against God and fear (Num. 14:9)—and they addressed them with words of exhortation coupled with encouragement to focus anew on the vision: "Only do not rebel against the LORD. And do not be afraid of the people of the land, because we will swallow them up. Their protection is gone, but the LORD is with us. Do not be afraid of them" (Num. 14:9).

In the same way, twenty-first century leaders of change will have to respond with firm persistence. They must not be quick to quit. Any time that they throw in the towel will be too soon. They need eyes to see the real issues of resistance such as rebellion and fear and identify them for the congregation. Finally, they must see even the most difficult situation as an opportunity to promote and cast a better vision for tomorrow.

At this point in the change process, Schaller asks, "How can the change be stabilized at this point of equilibrium to prevent slipping back to a former state of affairs, but not fixed so rigidly that the current effort at freezing will be a barrier to further change in the future?"[21] The best answer is to evaluate regularly all the programs of the church in light of the vision. Most programs in the church, such as the Sunday school, the choir, fund-raising, and so on, have a "shelf life" of eighteen to twenty-four months, after which they need to be changed or abandoned. For example, a church might want to add to or replace the Sunday school with a small group program. It may discontinue the choir and use the choir members in duets, trios, quartets, and other roles. Systematic evaluation helps prevent slippage and promote further change where needed. Critique the Sunday morning worship services weekly. The evaluative questions are: What did we do well, what did we not do well, and how can we do it better next time? Other ministries in the church should be critiqued at least monthly by those who are responsible for them.

9

The Tools of Change
The Change Agent's Toolbox

As he looked around the empty church sanctuary, Pastor Gary sensed several conflicting emotions. Excitement pumped through his veins. This was what he had been waiting for throughout his seminary days; this was what he had been planning for the last few months as he prayed and debated taking the pastorate of Chapel Hill Community Church. At the same instant, he sensed the butterflies of apprehension fluttering about and bumping back and forth between the walls of his stomach. Armed with a clear, significant vision, an initial plan to implement that vision, and the names of a few early innovators who would serve as potential allies in the church, he was about to commence the revitalization process.

Several days before, Pastor Gary and his family had arrived in the area and settled in a modest three-bedroom house located in a quiet suburb a few miles from the church. He had moved into his small office and somehow managed to find enough shelves for all his books. He viewed his books as tools to be used in ministry for the Lord. But his ministry toolbox contained other tools in addition to his books. He had intentionally collected a number of change principles that he would use at various stages as he cast a new vision and implemented his plan at Chapel Hill Community Church. He had gleaned these from his prior ministry experience, the experiences of others, and from books, articles, and tapes he had collected.

Every catalyst of intentional change needs a toolbox filled with various tools to accomplish revitalization. He views the process of

143

change (unfreezing, moving to a new level, and refreezing) much as an auto mechanic views the engine of a car. An automobile engine needs periodic adjustment and fine tuning throughout its life to run smoothly and efficiently. The change process requires the same, only the tools consist not of screwdrivers, a socket set, or special diagnostic equipment but of various practices of change. As the change agent leads the church through the change process, he will use these practices at various times in various places to keep the process running smoothly.

Prayer for Change

While prayer was mentioned in the last chapter, not enough can be said about the importance of prayer to the change process. Leaders must constantly remind themselves of the critical role prayer plays in revitalizing people. The battle over change is ultimately a spiritual not a physical battle being fought on spiritual grounds in the heavenlies, not between personalities in earthly church facilities. In Ephesians 6:10–20, Paul reminds us that we are involved in spiritual warfare against evil spiritual forces. A vital piece of the armor which God provides for every Christian is prayer. Paul writes: "And pray in the Spirit on all occasions with all kinds of prayers and requests. With this in mind, be alert and always keep on praying for all the saints" (Eph. 6:18).

A casual leafing through the Bible reveals that major events in Scripture are prefaced with prayer. In Nehemiah 1:5–11, upon hearing of the desperate situation of the Jews who had escaped and survived the captivity in Jerusalem, Nehemiah sat down, wept, and turned to God in a prayer of repentance and petition for his people. In Matthew 26:36–46, before being nailed to the cross, the Savior came with his disciples into the Garden of Gethsemane, fell with his face to the ground, and prayed concerning the Father's will and his disciples. Early in the Book of Acts, prior to the account of the tremendous expansion of the church, Luke provides a cameo appearance of the disciples in an upper room in Jerusalem. He writes, "They all joined together constantly in prayer, along with the women and Mary the mother of Jesus, and with his brothers" (Acts 1:14).

In John 15:5 the Savior reminds us that without him we can accomplish nothing of spiritual significance. To attempt church revitalization without these words emblazoned across the walls of your mind is to invite failure. Many wise change agents have a worn, ragged page where John 15 appears in their Bibles. Others have mounted it on a plaque on their office walls as a regular reminder of their insufficiency outside of Christ.

In his book *The Spirit of the Disciplines,* Dallas Willard underlines the importance of the spiritual disciplines to authentic Christian living. He divides them into the disciplines of abstinence and engagement. Under the disciplines of engagement is prayer. Willard writes: "Even when we are praying for or about things other than our own spiritual needs and growth, the effect of conversing with God cannot fail to have a pervasive and spiritually strengthening effect on *all* aspects of our personality. That conversation, when it is truly a conversation, makes an indelible impression on our minds, and our consciousness of him remains vivid as we go our way."[1] However, the other disciplines are vital to an intentional, significant prayer life as well. Willard writes, "But prayer will not be established in our lives as it must be for us to flourish, unless we are practicing other disciplines such as solitude and fasting."[2] While the change agent practices a vibrant prayer life, he would be wise to combine the discipline of prayer with the discipline of solitude as modeled by the Savior in Mark 1:35: "Very early in the morning, while it was still dark, Jesus got up, left the house and went off to a solitary place, where he prayed."

Faith for Change

In addition to prayer, another spiritual revitalization tool is faith. In a decade of megachange that stands on the brink of the third millennium A.D., God uses men and women of faith to breathe new life into plateaued and dying churches. At the dawn of the first millennium A.D., the Savior was impressed by men and women of faith as illustrated by the centurion in Matthew 8:8–10 and the Canaanite woman in Matthew 15:21–28. The Gentile centurion, a commander of one hundred men, merely uttered a command and soldiers jumped to comply. He came to Jesus to request healing for his paralyzed servant, yet he felt totally undeserving of the Savior's presence in his house. When Jesus heard this he was astonished and said, "I have not found anyone in Israel with such great faith." The Canaanite woman had to push through all kinds of obstacles to get to the Savior. He identified her faith as a "great faith" (Matt. 15:28). By way of stark contrast, his constant complaint with his so-called faithful Jewish disciples was their lack of faith. Numerous times the words "O ye of little faith!" echo through the pages of the Gospels.

How important is faith? According to the writer of Hebrews, "without faith it is impossible to please God" (Heb. 11:6). But this is a "tough faith" not an "easy faith" as promptly illustrated by Noah and Abraham in verses 7 and 8. Noah built without seeing. To trust God and build an ark put him at tremendous risk. If it had not rained, the ark would have served not to save his life but to scar his life. It would have been a perpetual reminder to him and all those around of personal failure. Abraham traveled without knowing. He heard God's call and struck out for places unknown. What if he had gotten lost or there had been no promised land? This kind of faith is "tough" because it makes such irrational, high-risk demands on the human intellect, which has grown accustomed to acting on the assurance of prior vision and knowledge. But leaders of change must learn to operate with the eyes of a Noah or an Abraham if they expect God to bless their ministries with life changes.

Questions of Change

The wise leader encourages change more by asking insightful questions than by offering directions or giving ultimatums. Like carbon on a spark plug, directions and ultimatums invite resistance. Questions serve leaders of intentional change as a tool to blow the carbon away for greater engine life and mileage. People who resist change and innovation are not thinking within the same paradigm as the change agent. Questions serve to catalyze and challenge the thinking process.

In the garden after the fall, God asked Adam, "Have you eaten from the tree that I commanded you not to eat?" Then he asked Eve, "What is this you have done?" He used these questions to pierce through their veneer of denial to expose their willful disobedience. The Savior was a master at the skillful use of questions to challenge the thought processes for the purpose of change. In dealing with the Pharisees in Matthew 22:41–46, he asked a series of logical questions, which led them to the irrefutable conclusion that the Messiah was both David's human descendant and Lord.

Questions encourage change in several ways. First, the new pastor in a church is allowed some naiveté. Consequently he can ask numerous dumb questions about the status quo, which most people will find unoffensive yet enlightening and convicting. Kouzes and Posner write, "By constantly asking people, 'Why do we do this, and why do we do that?' he will uncover some needed improvements in the organization."[3] Like a three-year-old child just discovering the world, he has permission to ask repeatedly, "Why?" Second, by skillfully asking the right questions, the change agent can challenge people to think along the same lines and come up with similar ideas or new ideas on their own. As long as the change agent does not mind who gets the credit, this grants people ownership of new, innovative ideas. Third, questions point people in the right direction. The Savior used this technique in the Garden of Gethsemane when he asked Peter and the disciples, "Could you not keep watch with me for one hour?" and later, "Are you still sleeping and resting?" His point was that they needed to stay awake so they would not fall into temptation (Matt. 26:41). A new pastor could ask, "Why is the paint peeling off the outside of the church's facility?" or "How long has the plumbing been clogged in the men's bathroom?"

The Terms of Change

Language is among the most powerful tools for expressing new and innovative ideas concerning change. Successful leaders use language in general and terms in particular that excite and motivate people. Therefore, those who lead their churches through the change process must pay particular attention to the terms they use. Deserving special attention is the word *change*.

Change means different things to different people, which involves the connotative not the denotative meaning of the word. The denotative meaning of a word is its dictionary meaning. The connotative meaning is the suggestive significance a word has to a particular person. Intrinsically, change is neither good nor bad but may be viewed as such according to an individual's experience with it. The word itself may conjure up good feelings or bad feelings according to a person's prior experience. Some who have experienced a new, life-changing ministry may view change with positive feelings of excitement and expectation. Others who value the past and life as it "should be" may view it with fear and suspicion.

Insightful pastors who lead those with a negative view toward change would be wise to use other words and various synonyms for change. In *Say No, Say Yes to Change*, Elaine Dickson warns: "But the fact remains that change, even in these positive references, is not always positive. *Change* remains what it is: a stark, even harsh and cold word. Change promises no respect for values. Change may help *or* hurt; it may hurt *and* help. Change may destroy *or* develop; it may destroy *and* develop."[4]

Dickson proceeds to offer some terms which tend to deflate the loaded, emotional energy surrounding the term *change*. She writes:

> Change by any other name appears easier to deal with. There are many words in our vocabulary which suggest change. A few of these are: *education, training, orientation, supervision, counseling, consulting,* and *parenting.* These terms imply that change will happen, and they carry essentially positive connotations. Because of the positive connotations of these words, these processes are seen as necessary and helpful.[5]

The New American Roget's College Thesaurus lists various synonyms for change under nouns, verbs, and adjectives. Some selected nouns: *alteration, diversification, variation, modification, substitution, modulation, and innovation.* Some verbs: *alter, vary, temper, modulate, diversify, qualify, turn the corner, modify, transform, innovate, recast, revamp, transpose, and reorganize.* Some adjectives: *altered, novel, variable, transitional, modifiable, and alternative.*[6] If the communicator of change leads in a potentially explosive change situation, he should review these lists and select several nouns, verbs, and adjectives to use in place of the word *change* to avoid needlessly offending the congregational hard-liners.

Communication for Change

Good communication is a tool that is critical to church revitalization no matter if the congregation is at the very beginning or well into the process. It is as important to the change process in the church body as the circulatory system is to the human body. Change in itself is such a threatening experience that it guarantees misinformation. Also, normal people want to know what is happening or else they become suspicious. By working hard at communicating well, the leader of transition keeps open the channels of communication and corrects any miscommunication between himself, other leaders, and the membership.

The problem is that the typical congregation communicates poorly if at all. And this problem is magnified in churches going through the change process, with the result that the process meets lots of resistance. Most in the church, including the pastor, are unaware of this. Ellis provides three safe, valid assumptions of communication for leaders in the change process:

1. Assume the message did not get through. It is estimated that 70 percent of what is transmitted is not received.
2. Assume that if it did get through, it was garbled either in transmission or in receiving.
3. Acknowledgment that the message was received does not necessarily imply acceptance or compliance.[7]

Leaders can accomplish good communication in several ways. First, they must listen as well as talk. Schaller writes that "active listening is one of the most important components for effecting a strategy of planned change within any organization."[8] In leading a church through the change process, pastors do a lot of talking; they must be prepared to do a lot of patient listening. People are more open to change when they feel they have had some say as to what is taking place in "their church." Most do not expect the church to agree with them entirely, but they do expect the church to give them the opportunity to speak and be heard.

Second, take advantage of every opportunity to communicate the vision and the plan. Gary McIntosh writes:

> Give people specifics. Explain how each person, class or group can contribute to the turnaround. Keep people informed by writing letters to their home. Use small group meetings or desserts where people may hear what steps are being taken for the future and have opportunity to ask questions. Make public all that is appropriate. Maintain a spirit of openness and vulnerability.[9]

Third, be alert to any misinformation in general and false rumors in particular. When leaders hear misinformation, they should attempt to discover the source of that information. They should track it back to its point of origin and correct it at that point. If the source is maliciously attempting to start false rumors, then he or she must be disciplined according to Matthew 18:15–19.

Fourth, communicate through periodic progress reports. People respond negatively when surprised. Schaller writes, "Most normal people need time to talk themselves into supporting a new idea."[10]

149

They may not like the idea at first, but given time they come to a point of acceptance. Therefore, wise leaders and long-range planning committees use periodic progress reports to minimize congregational surprises when the change is implemented or the final report is released.

Fifth, along with formal progress reports leaders of change may want to informally leak information as well. When meeting with various groups and individuals, they can release accurate information. This, too, gives people time to talk themselves into supporting new ideas and backing changes before they are announced publicly.

Finally, any communication of change must be positive. Communicate announcements, plans, progress reports, leaks, and so on in a positive context. Just as change agents must be characterized as positive people so must their communication. They emphasize the benefits of painting the foyer or remodeling the entire sanctuary. They find the plus in every change no matter how difficult the situation.

Committees for Change

In most churches the responsibility to plan and initiate change falls on the pastor and/or lay governing board. Schaller points out that this expectation is fraught with difficulties. One is that while theoretically the pastor is in a position to be the most effective initiator of planned change, the vast majority of pastors are unwilling or unable to accomplish this role. He estimates that at least 75 percent are not comfortable or effective in planned change situations. Some reasons are that they are not visionary, they cannot communicate a vision, they were not prepared in the dynamics of change in seminary, or the role of change agent is not compatible with the personality profiles of the majority of seminary graduates.[11]

Another difficulty is that most governing boards are standing committees. These committees are notorious for resisting change and opting for a maintenance mentality, which results in a maintenance ministry. Schaller writes:

> As will be pointed out in greater detail later, by nature standing committees predictably are more comfortable with continuity, stability, a ten-to-eighteen-month time frame, overseeing and maintaining continuing responsibilities, resisting change, and attracting

replacement members who are comfortable with the status quo. Rarely do standing committees either initiate or oversee major changes.[12]

According to Schaller, a solution, which is another tool for intentional change, is to create an ad hoc futures committee. He argues that the ad hoc study committee is a completely different breed of institutional creature from a standing committee and gives nine advantages of this committee for change.

In a transition situation where the pastor is a change agent, he could chair an ad hoc futures committee. The advantage is that the two would work together as a team. Otherwise they might work at odds to one another. While the committee is not the governing board of the church, it could consist of those on that board who are early adopters and other early adopters in the congregation.

One pastor in a small plateaued church grew tired of the response of his part-time lay-elder board to any proposals for change. The standard operating procedure of this standing committee was to talk any new proposals to death. Change frightened them, so they clung tenaciously to the status quo. When they attempted this with a proposal to add a new worship center to the present aging facility, the pastor wisely persuaded them to select and defer the matter to an ad hoc committee of older respected men in the congregation. The result was a new worship center which facilitated congregational growth.

Schaller summarizes the response of different kinds of church committees to change. He advises: "When someone proposes a new idea, decide how it should be handled. If you want it rejected, refer it to a standing committee. If you decide it needs refining and improving, send it to a special study committee. If it has obvious merit and deserves to be implemented, create a special ad hoc committee and direct its members to turn that new proposal into reality."[13]

Kinds of Change

Catalytic change agents lead congregations through the transition process more effectively when they understand the different kinds of change and how each affects people. The three kinds of change that implement revitalization are addition, subtraction, and replacement.

151

Change by addition creates a new situation by adding to the present church programs, schedules, and so on. It is a vital tool in the strategies of pastors who attempt to implement change in plateaued congregations. Schaller writes, "Sometimes the move up off a plateau in size can be accomplished slowly and gradually by a 'change-by-addition' strategy that leaves existing schedules, programs, groups, and classes undisturbed, but eventually that growth may require substantial changes in congregational life."[14] An example is the church that desires to center its prayer in a new, robust network of small groups rather than the current traditional Wednesday night prayer meeting. Instead of subtracting the sparsely attended prayer meeting from the schedule, the church treats it as a small group and gets on with the new small-groups program. The problem with this strategy is the accumulation of "excess baggage." Adding programs to existing programs has an effect on churches similar to adding layers upon layers of paint to the outside surface of the church's facility. Eventually the lower levels peel away taking the top levels with them.

Change by subtraction creates a new situation by scrapping the old one. It seldom occurs by itself and usually combines with change by addition. It is helpful periodically to scrape the barnacles off the side of the ministry ship. However, most churches replace the old with something new.

Change by subtraction and replacement is the key to revitalizing churches that are in decline. However, as Schaller notes, it is much more disruptive to congregational life than change by addition and will incur the greatest resistance.[15] To disband a traditional, declining Sunday school class that has been meeting since the birth of the church can devastate the few who remain faithful in attendance and someone like the founding teacher's affluent widow who views the class as a memorial to her husband. She may communicate her pain and displeasure and add the same to the church by withdrawing her tithe. Irving Bible Church saw the need to discontinue their Sunday evening service but replaced it with an active small-groups ministry. Other examples are the sale or demolition of the old facility and the purchase of a new one, the involuntary retiring of the elderly founding pastor and the hiring of his replacement. Both are necessary but extremely painful.

The pain involved in a change by subtraction and addition is the reason why it is easier to move a church off a plateau than to reverse a church in numerical decline. Older churches in the process of dying often find it less painful to close the front door than to initiate the kinds of changes necessary to revitalize and renew their ministry. Younger congregations are willing to do this but may drag their feet as they see cherished programs eliminated and replaced by new ones.

In spite of all the pain, there is hope for change by subtraction and addition. A powerful example is the struggle of the early church as it shed the binding shackles of Judaism for the authentic teachings of Christianity and grace. The struggle provided a constant storm of controversy between the Judaizers and the apostles and disciples. It dealt with such crucial issues as salvation and sanctification. Was a person saved by faith in Christ alone or by faith plus the keeping of the old laws and traditions? Was a person sanctified by grace alone or by keeping the commandments? The early church bravely and with integrity faced these storms of controversy. Not only did it survive them but it thrived and eventually conquered much of the Mediterranean world.

Levels of Change

Change takes place at different levels in people's lives. An awareness of each level serves as a tool to measure the effectiveness of change and to insure quality control. In *Say No, Say Yes to Change*, Dickson identifies three levels of change. The first level is compliance.[16] Change through compliance is forced change. People change because they feel they have to, not because they want to. Compliance change is caused by someone in authority or by an event beyond a person's control. The change takes place on the surface, not in the heart; therefore, its results are minimal. If it is to last for any length of time, it requires someone in authority to maintain it, or people soon revert back to their old ways. Thus it is very difficult to refreeze this change at the new level.

While change by compliance is necessary in such areas as law enforcement and raising small children, it is not appropriate for churches. It is the kind of change which is characteristic of legalistic churches. People change because of the rule of a dominant pastor who insists that everyone follow so-called biblical rules and regulations. Whenever he leaves or dies, most revert back to their old ways.

153

The second level is identification.[17] Identification change involves both individual initiative and the efforts of others. Dickson says that in identification change we identify two things: "Our own wants and needs for change, and attractive models (examples) who exhibit the change in which we are interested."[18] Either may come first, and the process may be conscious or unconscious.

An example is the pastor who desires to revitalize a dying church. He attends a pastors' conference put on by a successful megachurch in a different part of the country. When he returns home, he attempts to apply what he has learned from the megachurch to his own backyard. The fact that his community is different from that of the megachurch may or may not be a consideration.

Identification change is usually moderate change and much more preferable to compliance change. It is most effective when the conditions of the model church reflect those in the struggling church. However, this is rare. Leaders who attempt to learn from excellent models need to look for the transferable, biblical, and practical principles. The model's programs and practices may be helpful, but the leader must be prepared to innovate his own, which are more indigenous to his community. Otherwise, identification is no more than surface change. The tenure of identification change is in direct proportion to the change agent's abilities to implement the new ministry principles.

The third level of change is internalization.[19] It does not depend on either an external authority to keep it frozen in place or a significant model to motivate its presence. It takes place below the surface in the heart. Internalization change accomplishes maximum change and takes place because people want it and incorporate it into their lives. Dickson writes: "We believe in, feel strongly about, value, and decide to change to the new condition. We act out of our own inner commitment to the change."[20]

An example of internalization change is conversion and sanctification. When a person accepts Christ as Savior, God comes into his or her life and accomplishes an eternal, irrevocable change from the spiritual perspective. In 2 Corinthians 5:17 Paul writes, "Therefore, if anyone is in Christ, he is a new creation; the old is gone, the new has come!" Once an individual accepts Christ, the challenge is to grow in Christ-likeness, which is sanctification. This is a spiritual, experiential change that takes place over the lifetime of the Christian. Paul describes this change process in 2 Corinthians 3:18: "And we, who with unveiled faces all reflect the Lord's glory, are being transformed into his likeness with ever-increasing glory, which comes from the Lord, who is the Spirit."

Leaders of intentional change work with both the tools of identification and internalization change. Consequently, as they lead their ministries through the transformation process, a knowledge of these levels of change will help them to determine if they are accomplishing their desired results. They also serve as tools of quality control. Most likely, change will occur on all three levels. However, the majority of change must reflect identification and internalization, not compliance, if quality change is to occur. Otherwise, the entire change process, like an automobile engine, must be overhauled and adjusted accordingly.

Part 4

The Product of Change

Seeing Established Churches Reach Their Goal of Change

10

The Future Church
A New Face for the Church

Pastor Gary found himself dreaming a lot about the future of Chapel Hill Community Church, which is characteristic of most visionaries. A lot had happened in the short time since he had arrived there. God was using him to lead the ministry in a new direction. As he had anticipated, three of the four board members were responsive to his vision for the ministry's future and were open to change. Many in the congregation had become dissatisfied with the status quo and were excited about the new vision. The plan, with minor corrections, was being implemented faster than he had imagined. Also, he had recruited a number of men both young and old as allies to help lead and implement new ministry programs.

The sanctuary boasted a new coat of paint as the result of the smoke damage from the fire. However, it was in need of other repairs as well, so the church voted to remodel a significant portion of the sanctuary even though it was not in the budget. The new look delighted most of the people and instilled a sense of pride, which prompted them to invite a number of their churched and unchurched friends, some of whom trusted in the Savior.

Pastor Gary and some of his key people examined and visited several revitalized and new, cutting-edge churches that God was blessing. More important, they spent several months studying and discussing various biblical principles of the church found throughout the New Testament. They were amazed and delighted at Pastor Gary's knowledge of the Scriptures. Consequently, a clear, concise picture of the future Chapel Hill developed in their minds. In essence, this picture focused on seven key ingredients. In the age of megachange, they are seven biblical, foundational principles that are crucial to any church whether newly birthed or long established. These formed the basic direction in which Chapel Hill would move.

A Great Commission Vision

The leader who attempts to take a church through preplanned change must have a significant, challenging vision so that both he and the church know where they are going. But he cannot opt for just any vision. It must be a single, clear vision that finds its source in the Scriptures.

A Single, Clear Vision

Most churches respond in one of three ways to the concept of vision. The majority have no vision. If you ask the pastor or the board where the ministry will be two to five years later, they shrug their shoulders, look puzzled, and scratch their heads. These are passive churches that are going nowhere. Like ships without a compass, they wander across the ocean with no port in sight.

Some churches have multiple visions. They move in several different directions at the same time. One board member envisions a Christian school. A wealthy member sees a new facility as a memorial to his departed mother. The chairman of the board wants to support numerous missionaries overseas. Are not multiple visions better than no vision? The problem is that multiple visions produce unhappy people who split churches.

Finally, some churches own a single, clear vision. A problem exists if it is the wrong vision. These have become specialized churches in an age of specialization. One is known in the community for its great preacher, another for its family ministry, a third for its pastoral care, and a fourth for its choir or great Bible teaching. The problem is that these churches can cater to a consumer mentality: If your church does not meet your present needs, then shop around until you find one that does.

The Great Commission

Peter Drucker states that every business must ask itself several vital questions. The first is: What business are you in? While the church is a body, not a business, it should regularly ask itself the same question. What has Christ commissioned us to accomplish in this world? What is his vision for the church? The biblical answer is always the Great Commission. But what is the Great Commission? Three ingredients make up the Great Commission vision.

PURSUIT

The first ingredient is the intentional pursuit of lost people. It is found in the word *go* in Matthew 28:19 and Mark 16:15. The term is clarified and expanded as a theme in Luke's Gospel. Representative is Luke 19:1–10, the story of Zacchaeus.[1] The key verse is Luke 19:10, where the Savior states that his mission was "to seek" and "to save" the lost. In *The Expositor's Bible Commentary*, Walter Liefeld writes: "Verse 10 could well be considered the 'key verse' of Luke. . . . The verse itself expresses the heart of Jesus' ministry as presented by Luke, both his work of salvation and his quest for the lost."[2]

The heart of Jesus' ministry is found in the two infinitives *to seek* and *to save*. They are key to the structure of verses 1–10. Verses 1–7 comprise the seeking section and verses 8–9 the saving section. In verses 1–7, the Savior intentionally pursues Zacchaeus, who is an irreligious Jew. In verses 8–9, he saves him.

The intentional pursuit of the irreligious or unchurched continues to be the vision of the Savior and thus of the church in the twenty-first century. America is no longer the churched culture of the 1940s and 1950s. It has become the unchurched culture of the 1980s and 1990s and the church's mission field. Callahan writes: "Statistical research, analysis of this culture, and long-range projections all clearly indicated that ours is no longer a churched culture. Study after study and the steady decline of many mainline denominations confirm this fact. We are clearly and decisively entering the mission field of the 1990s."[3]

Unchurched people will not come to us. Callahan writes: "Within the broad-based culture after World War II, people held the value that church was important. . . . People sought the church out and self-initiated their own participation. It was 'the thing to do' to go to church."[4] All that has changed. If we expect to change them, we, like the Savior, must go to them.

However, on occasion some will come back for a visit when they marry or begin a family. Gallup labels this the "life cycle effect": The first generation unchurched left the church in their late teens or early twenties but return in their late twenties.[5] The crucial question for the church, therefore, is, What will they find when they return for a second look? They want orthodox, biblical Christianity, for many are in search of truth. But it must be wrapped in a culturally relevant package, or they will walk out again. Callahan observes, "The loss and decline should be teaching us something. . . . In a clear sense, I think this is God's way of teaching us that what we have been doing no longer works. Ultimately, we will continue to lose members until we figure that out."[6]

This means the church will have to change. If it is serious about Christ's mandate, it must endure the pain of change and become relevant to life in the 1990s and the twenty-first century. It is the choice between life and death.

EVANGELISM

The second ingredient of the Great Commission is evangelism. Great Commission churches make evangelism a high priority. They do not simply talk about evangelism, they are doing evangelism. They do not give testimony to one or two people coming to faith every other year; rather, numerous people give testimony to their having come to the Savior each year, with the result that these churches are growing numerically through conversion growth not transfer growth. They believe that a church that is not significantly involved in evangelism has lost its purpose.

Several qualities distinguish these Great Commission churches. First, they are not mentally locked into a single style of evangelism. For most the style is more relational (witnessing to a friend) than confrontational (witnessing to a complete stranger) but does not exclude the latter. Next, their motives are based not on guilt but on gratitude. They do not evangelize because someone has made them feel guilty if they do not, but because they want to see people accept Christ. The motivation is based on grace not legalism. Finally, their methods are many not few. They know that in fishing for men they must put lots of hooks in the water, for it takes all kinds of methods to reach all kinds of people.

EDIFICATION

The third ingredient of the Great Commission is edification. Great Commission churches are characterized by more than pursuing and evangelizing lost people. They do not win people to Christ and then abandon them. They understand that they are working within a small window of time. If new believers are not discipled soon after conversion, the window of interest closes, and they join the ranks of nominal Christianity. Therefore, these churches work hard to equip and disciple new believers so that they pursue Christ-likeness (Eph. 4:11–16).

A Strong Servant Leader

What does a change agent look like? A person who desires to lead an established church through the change process must have several critical features as part of his makeup.

A Leader

First, he must be a leader.[7] I define a Christian leader as a godly person (character) who knows where he is going (vision) and has followers (influence). This definition has three elements. The first is character. Godly character forms the foundation of Christian leadership. Beginning in the home (1 Tim. 3:4–5), it earns credibility and trust that is vital to any relationship. In light of the morality problem plaguing Christian leadership in the 1980s and 1990s, people today are asking if their leaders can be trusted. The leaders of twenty-first century churches must make spiritual formation a daily priority in their lives. The people who know them best must be convinced that they are authentic men of God as described in 1 Timothy 3:1–13 and Titus 1:5–9.

The second element of leadership is vision. Not only do people ask if their leader can be trusted, they want to know where he is going before they will follow him. There are two kinds of vision. One is personal-ministry vision. It is the future ministry direction of a person's life as based on his divine design. This was covered in more detail in chapter 3. The other is organizational or institutional vision, covered in chapter 8. It directly concerns the vision of the church, which is the Great Commission as discussed above. An important factor for maximum effectiveness in ministry is that the vision of the church align itself most closely with the leader's personal vision. A discrepancy in this area results in ministry burnout.

The third element of leadership is influence. Good leaders exert a strong, godly influence, which attracts followers. If a person says, "I'm a leader!" but turns around and no one is following, then he is not a leader. As someone once said, "He's simply taking a walk."

The way a Christian leader influences people is through a combination of his character and vision. People who exude both Christlike character and cast clear, significant visions attract committed followers.

A Strong Leader

Second, the change agent must be a strong leader.[8] One of the reasons so many of the churches in America are struggling is because pastors are not exercising strong, proactive leadership.

THE PROBLEM OF COLEADERSHIP

The problem many churches face at the end of the twentieth century is the struggle between pastors and lay governing boards over who will lead the church. In most cases, the boards have won, and the churches are led by multiple lay consensus or coleadership. This is the general result of an antiauthoritarian mood among church members, the promotion of a passive "enabler" model for professional leadership, and the church renewal movement of the 1960s and 1970s that missed the importance of having a full-time professional leader at the helm.

Full-time pastors are best qualified to lead for two reasons. One is time. A pastor's week easily consumes fifty to sixty hours. Consequently, he is immersed in the ministry process. He is the one who knows the organization inside and out. He has the very pulse of the church at his fingertips. While they may prove to be very capable, godly leaders, part-time lay volunteers do not have this kind of exposure to the ministry and are not able to be as sensitive to the direction and leadership needs of the church, even the small church. Time constraints will not allow it. The other reason is training. In addition to time in ministry, pastors are trained for their ministry and have a wealth of information and contacts from which to draw.[9] Lay board members do not have this privilege. Their schedules are filled up with business and family responsibilities that leave them little time to read the professional literature or become acquainted with the new church paradigms God is blessing in the 1990s and the twenty-first century.

THE ARGUMENT FOR STRONG LEADERSHIP

The solution to the problem of coleadership is strong pastoral leadership. Pastors need to be active not passive leaders. This does not mean that others are not involved in leadership. It does mean that the pastor functions on the team as the point person or leader of leaders. There are several arguments for strong pastoral leadership.

The first argument is theological. Where two or more persons serve together for any period of time, one must assume the position of primary leader. This is reflected in 1 Corinthians 11:3 where Christ is the head of man, man is the head of the woman, and, most important, God (the Father) is the head of Christ. While Scripture teaches that all three persons of the Godhead are equal in essence, the Father assumes the position of headship in terms of their function. If the Trinity, as a perfect leadership team, has a head, then it appears all the more necessary that church boards should have a head or leader of leaders as well.

The second argument is biblical. A number of individuals exercised strong leadership in the Scriptures. The classic example would be the Savior with his disciples. Another is Peter, who was always mentioned first in lists of the apostles and who was the chief spokesman and preacher in the Book of Acts. Third is James, who was the leader of the Jerusalem church.

The third argument is practical. All men are not created equal in their leadership abilities. Some have the gift of leadership (Rom. 12:8) and more knowledge and experience than others. The argument is to put these gifted people in the point positions and let them function as leaders of leaders.

A Strong Servant Leader

The third critical feature of the leader is servanthood. The agent of change combines strong leadership with the quality of a servant's heart. This can be compared to three other kinds of leadership.

One is absolute leadership. This is leadership by a dictator or a tyrant and often is an overreaction to coleadership. The dictator rules with an iron fist and has no accountability. He does not care for the sheep but insists they care for him. In Mark 10:42, the Savior says this is a characteristic of pagan leadership: "You know that those who are regarded as rulers of the Gentiles lord it over them, and their high officials exercise authority over them."

The second is coleadership. This is leadership by consensus and is characteristic of churches led by voluntary, part-time lay boards without a leader of leaders. It has developed as an overreaction to absolute leadership and tends to be passive. Peter Wagner offers two cogent observations regarding coleadership. The first is that "the plurality-of-elders structure is good for small churches and non-growing churches. But as a church gains growth momentum and becomes larger, the system becomes more dysfunctional."[10] The second is that "in almost all of the plurality-of-elder churches which are growing, a top leader has emerged even though one was not supposed to. Some of the strongest leaders I know say 'I don't lead' and go ahead and do it."[11]

The third is biblical leadership. If a man desires to lead a church, he must have a servant's heart. In Mark 10:45, Christ says, "For even the Son of Man did not come to be served but to serve, and to give his life as a ransom for many." But what is a servant leader? A popular misconception is that he is a passive person who serves as a "doormat." The biblical example is the Savior who was no "doormat." In his leadership of the disciples, he was definitely in charge, a leader of leaders. At the same time, he passionately loved these men and eventually gave his life for them.

A servant leader, then, is a person who is willing to take charge and exercise strong leadership when necessary. At the same time, this person does not lead from personal interest or ambition but is looking out for the interests of his people (Phil. 2:3–7). The attitude is not that of being served but of service to others. Oswald Sanders states it well when he writes, "Jesus did not have in mind *acts of service,* for those can be performed from very dubious motives. He meant the *spirit of servanthood,* which He expressed when He claimed, 'I am among you as He that serves.'"[12] He then pulls several characteristics of servanthood from Isaiah 42:1–5 that previews the Messiah's leadership. One is voluntary dependence on the Father by submitting to his will (v. 1). Another is the approval of the Father, not the approval of men (v. 1). A third is modesty as exemplified by a quiet and unobtrusive spirit (v. 2). A fourth is empathy toward those who are weak or wounded (v. 3). A fifth is a spirit of optimism that inspires followers (v. 4). And the fifth is the anointing of the Holy Spirit who supplies the supernatural power to lead (v. 5).[13]

Servant leadership is distinguishable from absolute leadership and coleadership. Unlike the dictator, the servant leader does not callously run over his people, but he listens to and cares about them. Unlike coleadership, the servant leader is proactive and willing to step forward and lead. While he may have strong opinions, he does not force them on others but listens and gives cogent reasons for his conclusions. Ultimately, the board looks to him for leadership because of his wisdom and humble, Christ-like character.

A Well-mobilized Lay Army

In 1 Corinthians 12, Paul compares the church to a vibrant, fully functioning human body. Just as it is critical that all the parts of the human body be present and functioning, so it is in the life of the church. This is the mandate to mobilize the laity. Christ's desire for his church is that all its members function actively. But a quick glance at the typical church reveals that what Christ desires and reality are not the same.

The Problem

The great tragedy in many churches is that most Christians are not involved in any ministry of the church. This is an unemployment problem. Not that people are looking for jobs; just the opposite. There are lots of jobs, but no one is rushing to fill them.

John Maxwell, the pastor of Skyline Wesleyan Church in San Diego, California, has developed the 20–80 principle. He says that 20 percent of the people in a typical church are doing 80 percent of the ministry of the church. Thus, Maxwell believes that on average 80 percent of the people in American churches are not using their gifts and abilities for the Savior. Win Arn believes it is closer to 70 percent overall. He writes that "growing churches average 55 percent of their membership involved in a role or task; declining churches average only 27 percent."[14]

According to George Gallup, Maxwell and Arn are too optimistic. He believes that 10 percent of the people are doing 90 percent of the ministry. Of the 90 percent, approximately 50 percent say they will not become involved, and 40 percent say they will if asked.

Larry Richards and his colleagues conducted a survey in which they asked 5,000 pastors what the greatest needs were for strengthening the church. The response: "On a scale of five from a twenty-five-item list, nearly 100 percent gave a first or second priority to 'getting my lay people involved as ministering men and women.'"[15]

The Reasons

While there are numerous reasons why Christians are unemployed in their churches, two stand out. One is a lack of people's confidence in their abilities to serve Christ effectively. While they may feel totally adequate in the marketplace, many feel totally inadequate in the church. This is characteristic of preboomers who grew up during the Great Depression and World War II. The result is they leave the ministry to the professionals. ("Let Rev. Smith do it. After all, that's what we hired him for in the first place.")

Another is "recruitment wars." This is a recruitment process based on emotion and/or coercion. People grow weary of "tear-filled" sermons or pastoral "arm twisting." For example, one person complained, "When the pastor began to cry because six-year-old Mary Smith would have no Sunday school teacher, I gave in, and I don't even like kids." Another lamented, "The pastor kept bugging me. Every time I saw him, he would pressure me to help. He even called me at home and at work." In addition, some churches have no recruitment process. The pastor depends on a yearly sermon on spiritual gifts to fill the empty spaces in the program, and it never works.

A Solution

The obvious solution is to equip and mobilize lay people for ministry in their churches. But most pastors and church workers know this. The question is how to accomplish it. The answer is an assessment program, and a good one has three phases.[16]

First is the education phase. Its purpose is to help lay people discover their divine designs for their unique ministries. The education phase has two parts. One is instruction of believers about spiritual and natural gifts, passion, temperament, leadership styles, and so on. To develop confidence, it also communicates that all Christians are believer-priests (1 Peter 2:5–9; Rev. 1:6) who are indwelled by the Holy Spirit (1 Cor. 6:19), and that he, in turn, provides the power necessary to accomplish their ministry (Eph. 3:16, 20). The other part is evaluation. Each person listens with an "evaluative ear" and attempts to determine his exact design. This may include the use of evaluative tools such as a spiritual-gifts or temperament inventory.[17]

Second is the consultation phase. The purpose of this phase is to provide people with personal help in determining their design for

168

ministry. This is accomplished through a professional staff person in larger churches and a trained lay person in smaller churches. The consultant is available to help individuals determine or confirm their designs, administer assessment tools, and answer any questions.

Third is the mobilization phase. Its purpose is to place believers in their ministry niche either within or outside the walls of the church. The consultant is aware of the divine designs of the people in the church and all the ministry needs and opportunities of the church. He or she serves to match the right person with the right ministry, which results in happier, fulfilled servants who experience little burnout. If there is no ministry opportunity for a particular person within the existing church programs, then the church must decide whether to use that person to start a new ministry.

A Culturally Relevant Ministry

Megachange has become a way of life in the 1990s and early twenty-first century. The problem for most typical churches is that they have not made the adjustments necessary to remain biblically relevant to the culture. Consequently, the unchurched baby boomers and busters view them as out of touch and will have nothing to do with them. Under their breath they remark, "Everybody knows a dinosaur when they see one!"

A culturally relevant ministry is the result of understanding the theology of change. A correct theology of change focuses on the issue of knowing what a church can and must not change and then making the appropriate applications.

The Issue

Any church that desires to be relevant and reach its generation for Christ must determine what can and cannot change in terms of its ministry. The issue is one of functions versus forms of ministry. The evangelical church appears greatly confused over this issue. In general, it does not seem to be aware of this distinction and treats both its functions and forms as equally binding on its people.

Changing What It Believes

The functions of ministry form the very basis for which the ministry exists. They make up *what* the church does. In the evangelical church, these functions must be derived from the Scriptures, and are actually the principles of faith. Some examples are evangelism, worship, prayer, the proclamation of the Word (whether preaching or teaching), confession, the ordinances, and others.

Since these functions are based on Scripture, they are eternal and unchangeable. Christ's church will forever seek to base its ministry on them. In fact, they form the essential ingredients that make up any and all ministries of the church.

Churches of liberal persuasion differ with evangelical churches on this issue. They do not view the Bible as teaching eternal and unchangeable truth for Christians, whether they lived in the first century or the twenty-first century. Consequently, they have attempted to remain culturally relevant by changing the functions of the faith. One example of this in the decade of the 1990s is the attempt in several liberal denominations to ordain homosexuals for the ministry. It is important to note that this strategy of changing belief has not worked, as evidenced in chapter 2 by the significant decline in membership of the mainline denominations across America.

Changing What It Does

The forms of ministry are built on the functions of ministry. They are the principles being worked out in the ministry of a church. They affect *how* and even *when* a church does *what* it does. For example, evangelism is a ministry function that is essential to every church. However, there are different forms that evangelism can take. Those with the gift of evangelism often use a confrontational style. Others prefer a more relational style such as friendship evangelism.

Scripture grants the church much freedom for the forms of its ministry. In 1 Corinthians 9:19–23, Paul writes that though he had certain rights within the realm of his Christian liberty, he was willing to set them aside to reach the lost people of his generation. It is important to note that he does not advocate disobedience to biblical imperatives. He discusses various Christian liberties allowed by those imperatives. According to verse 20, he became like those under the law to reach them with the gospel. These were the religious, lost Jews of the first century who faithfully attended the temple services but rejected the Messiah. They parallel the religious lost people of today who attend church but reject Christ. In verse

21, he became like those who were not under the law to reach them as well. These were nonreligious Gentiles who are similar to today's unchurched generation. Wherever Scripture permitted, Paul was willing to adapt to the culture and practices of people, whether under the law or not, to win their lives for Christ.

The Application

How does this apply to change and the traditions and practices of the local church? First, the traditional church needs to distinguish between what is actually biblical and binding and what is not. To accomplish this it is imperative that pastors and church leaders know their Bibles well. The problem is that far too many people in evangelical churches confuse temporal forms with biblical functions. For them, to advocate a more contemporary style of worship is synonymous to ripping the Book of Romans out of the Bible.

Second, traditional churches must be willing to flex their cultural practices when they are no longer relevant. This involves an outward as well as an inward focus. They must put other people, lost people, before themselves. This could mean wearing sweaters instead of suitcoats on Sunday morning, developing a contemporary worship service for the boomer and buster generations, or scheduling a special service for non-Christians at a time more convenient than the members are used to. These are examples of forms that are flexible and not mandated by Scripture.

Third, these churches must exegete their culture as well as their Bibles. They need to be students of the "world out there" (the culture of the community) and the "world in here" (the culture of the church). The result is that they will have the information necessary to apply biblical truth in an authentic, relevant manner. This was the practice of the men of Issachar who in the Old Testament were described as those who "understand their times and know what Israel should do" (1 Chron. 12:32).

Finally, the traditional church should constantly evaluate its ministry forms. Outside of biblical functions, there should be no "sacred cows." Every ministry has a "shelf life" ranging from eighteen to twenty-four months. Evaluation prevents ministry forms from becoming institutionalized and needlessly perpetuated. It removes them from the shelf before they spoil and go bad. This is agreed on at the inception of a ministry and becomes the responsibility of those who conduct the various ministries of the church. An example is the church that insists on a Wednesday night prayer meeting that most people have stopped attending. Prayer could take place at other better attended programs such as small group meetings.

A Holistic, Authentic Worship

One important area of ministry that is receiving much attention in typical churches is worship. The Pepsi generation of believers is clashing with the Truman generation over the issue of worship. What is the problem? A good example is the relevant preaching of Bill Hybels, the pastor of Willow Creek Community Church outside Chicago. He studies and spends time with the non-Christians in the Chicago community. Consequently, when he preaches, he applies the truth of Scripture to the specific needs of non-Christian attendees.

The Problem of Inauthentic Worship

As the twentieth century draws toward a close, far too many traditional churches have missed the importance of authentic worship in the lives of their people. Our God is worthy of our worship, and authentic worship is an active response to him in that we focus on him and acknowledge his worth. It consists of such elements as adoration, confession, thanksgiving, prayer, proclamation, and so on. It is well-planned, never boring, and captures the congregation's attention. People leave with a sense of having been in the life-changing presence of God. To be specific, not much authentic worship is taking place in many evangelical churches. What is an example of typical, inauthentic worship? Allen and Borror write:

> The prelude was played on a very fine organ, but no one paid much attention. The bulletin gave no clue as to where the congregation was heading, so the organist could not have known what was appropriate. The verbal part of the service began with an aggressive reading of a Psalm of praise, followed by an impromptu, urgent plea for Sunday school teachers given by a well-intentioned lay leader who really needed help. He tacked on an immediate appeal for two or three to come now to rescue a class of junior boys running around in the parking lot! This was followed by a greeting from a recently returned missionary who was doing a great work, but

needed (and took) too long to tell about it, frustrating himself as well as others. We then came to the opening hymn (twenty minutes into the service) which had nothing to do with either the teaching or missions. After the hymn, the Scripture was to be read (it was related to the hymn theme) but it was dropped due to the lateness of the hour.[18]

From God's perspective, this is offering up blemished lambs to the unblemished lamb of Calvary. From a lay perspective this kind of worship is totally inadequate to transform lives.

In far too many evangelical churches, Christians live and die for the sermon. Worship is viewed as the "warmup" before the big game, or the soup and salad before the main course. Allen and Borror comment:

It follows that as pastors, we evangelicals have not been much concerned with worship either. In many of our circles the Sunday morning event is considered a "preaching service" in spite of the fact that the official title in the bulletin reads "Morning Worship." Viewing the preacher's singular act of proclamation as significantly more important than the entire congregation's acts of adoration, praise, confession, thanksgiving, and dedication is espousing an expensive heresy which may well be robbing many a church of its spiritual assets.[19]

When it is not valued, worship is poorly done, predictable, boring, and ultimately irrelevant. Rather than attract people *to* the Savior, insipid worship distracts them *from* the Savior. The unchurched pay a visit and vow never to return, saying they have more important things to do with their time. As soon as our young people complete high school, they drop out and join the ranks of the unchurched, vowing never to be bored again. But what can leaders do who find themselves trapped in the web of boring worship?

A Philosophy of Authentic, Holistic Worship

The solution to this problem is to change to worship that is both authentic and holistic. Authentic worship not only praises God, but it benefits the worshiper. The result is holistic worship—that which has an impact on the total person—the worshiper's intellect, emotions, and will.

Holistic worship can have a tremendous impact on God's people by renewing their spirits and bringing them to a fresh commitment of their lives to the Savior. In fact, Romans 12:1 says this should be a result of authentic worship. Would it not greatly honor the Savior if each week the worship services magnified him to the extent that people's souls were refreshed and they recommitted their lives to him?

For holistic worship to occur, the worship experience first affects the mind so that believers understand biblically what they are singing, saying, and doing. Next, it touches the emotions so that worship impacts the affective aspect of their souls as well as the cognitive. David repeatedly illustrated the emotional impact of worship in the Psalms. Jesus demonstrated it intensely while praying in the garden before the crucifixion. He taught that Christians must love God with more than the intellect: "Love the Lord your God with all your heart and with all your soul and with all your mind" (Matt. 22:37). When worship affects both the intellect and the emotions, it can result in a life-changing decision for God which accomplishes a Romans 12:1 experience (figure 13). God uses the emotions in worship to touch the depths of people's souls and change their hearts so that they renew themselves for his service.

The Implementation of Authentic, Holistic Worship

What practices lead to the renewal of worship and encourage authentic, holistic worship among the people in evangelical churches? First, leaders must be worshipers. It takes a worshiper to lead worshipers. Therefore, leaders themselves must develop as authentic worshipers of Christ. This process begins in solitary, daily times with God. However, that which is private and personal throughout the week becomes public during congregational worship once a week. Obviously, this involves much more than standing and leading singing, as is required of various pastors in some small, traditional churches. It involves leading the congregation in times of corporate adoration, confession, thanksgiving, and prayer.

Second, worship must be culturally relevant. It is true that cultural relevance varies from age to age and community to community. The congregation that desires to reach the younger generation for Christ must consider implementing some form of contemporary worship. Not to do so is to fail to attract the younger generation and to lose those who are present. This is best accom-

Figure 13
Authentic, Holistic Worship

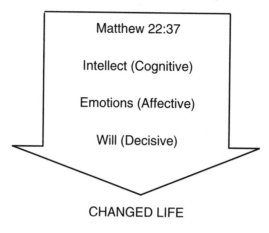

Matthew 22:37

Intellect (Cognitive)

Emotions (Affective)

Will (Decisive)

CHANGED LIFE

Romans 12:1

plished in most older, traditional congregations not by dramatically changing the traditional service but by adding a second contemporary service at an earlier hour.[20] Another option is to plant a contemporary church with a contemporary worship format.

Third, worship must be done well. Regardless of the style of worship, poor worship is never an adequate substitute for the real thing. Scripture teaches a theology of excellence (Lev. 22:20–22; Eph. 6:5–8; Col. 3:23–24). Even at the judgment seat of Christ we will be judged according to the quality of our works (1 Cor. 3:13). When applied to worship, God wanted his people to offer their best when they worshiped him (Lev. 22:20–22). This means that the people involved in worship cannot "fly by the seat of their pants." If the soloist did not take time to rehearse, then he or she should wait until another time. If the pianist is less than mediocre, sing a cappella. If an instrument is not tuned, do not attempt to play it.

Fourth, worship requires a proper environment. Authentic worship can take place in the worst of environments. Some early saints worshiped in caves and in prisons. However, this need not be the case in most local church facilities in the 1990s. Churches have a tendency to miss the little things that make a big difference in the quality of their worship time. They must give more attention to such matters as the lighting, sound equipment, seating, acoustics, placement of instruments, and other matters.

Finally, worship can be creative and innovative. Baby boomers and busters are "turned off" when worship is boring and predictable. Thus, churches should feel free to explore and seek fresh insights into various forms of worship. Innovative worship may include skits, drama, audio-visual presentations, creative dance, the use of video in preaching, and other creative forms.

A Biblical, Culturally Relevant Evangelism

The statistics indicate that not much evangelism is taking place in the typical American church. If the ministry of evangelism is a vital sign for the church body, then its health is poor at best. In his book *A New Look at Church Growth*, Floyd Bartel writes, "95 percent of all Christians in North America will not win one person to Christ in their entire lifetime."[21] Barna writes, "In the past seven years, the proportion of adults who have accepted Christ as their personal Savior (34 percent) has not increased."[22]

The Problem

Several reasons account for the church's lapse in the area of evangelism. The first is that far too may churches resemble a holy huddle. Most Christians do not socialize with non-Christians. If you were to take a picture of the average believer and his friends, there would be no non-Christians in the crowd. Joe Aldrich says that two years after a person comes to faith, he has shed his non-Christian friends. This was not the case with the Savior, for much of his time was given to sinners and publicans (Luke 5:27–32; 15:1–2; 19:1–10).

The second reason for little evangelism is that churches maintain culturally irrelevant methods. Evangelistic methods that worked in the 1940s and 1950s are not effective in the 1990s. The primary difference is that the old methods depended on some prior knowledge of spiritual truth that the people had gained attending a church. The methods for the present do not have this advantage, because most boomers and busters have a limited knowledge of the Bible and Christianity.

The third reason for little evangelism is false assumptions. The traditional church has misunderstood the unchurched generation in several ways. First, it has missed the shift from a churched culture to an unchurched culture and does not realize that the latter are no longer pursuing the church. You cannot hang a welcome sign out front and expect people to flock to the church. Second, it does not realize that unchurched people are secular not Judeo-Christian. There is little evidence in the second half of this century of the strong Judeo-Christian influence that characterized the first half of the century. Next, it does not understand that the unchurched person is more concerned with the here and now than the hereafter. Fourth, it has missed the fact that unchurched people are process not event oriented. Consequently, the chances of a person coming to Christ using a short-term, "cold turkey" approach are not as good as with a long-term-relationship approach to evangelism.

The Solution

The solution is a biblically based evangelism that is supersensitive to the culture. A problem for many people in the church is that they have mentally locked into a stereotypical form of evangelism: confrontational evangelism. And most are not interested in what they perceive to be a "Gunfight at the O.K. Corral" approach.

A biblically based evangelism paints an entirely different picture through numerous styles for accomplishing evangelism. In his book *Honest to God?*, Bill Hybels describes six styles of evangelism from the Bible. The first is the confrontational style demonstrated by Peter in his Pentecost sermon in Acts 2, where three thousand Jews responded to Christ. The second is the intellectual style used by Paul in Acts 17:3, which consisted of his "explaining and proving" that Christ was the Messiah. The third is the testimonial style used by the blind beggar in John 9. Christ had restored his sight, and he responded by giving testimony to all who inquired as to what had changed his life. The fourth is the relational style of the demon-possessed man in Mark 5. His response to Christ's work was to want to follow him wherever he traveled. Instead, the Savior instructed him to return to his family and use that natural person-to-person relationship for evangelism. The fifth is the invitational style used by the Samaritan woman, who, after she spoke with Christ, invited her fellow Samaritans to come listen to him (John 4:39). Sixth is the serving style of Dorcas as demonstrated by her life in Acts 9.[23]

Effective evangelism uses methods that fit the contemporary culture of the community. In America in the 1960s and 1970s, good

177

evangelism methods consisted of city-wide crusades, "Jesus saves" bumper stickers, road signs demanding that people everywhere repent, and door-to-door witnessing. Today few attend evangelistic crusades except those put on by the Billy Graham Evangelistic Association. People laugh at bumper stickers and religious road signs; they think they are weird. Door-to-door witnessing still works in blue collar communities and some parts of the inner city, but has proved less effective in suburbia and affluent communities. These less effective methods have been replaced in the 1990s by home Bible discussions and special seeker-targeted services and programs. And this will probably change in the twenty-first century.

A Robust Network of Small Groups

The baby boom generation has been described as "a relationally vacuous generation struggling in their ability to form lasting relationships."[24] In *Christianity Today,* Paula Rinehart reports: "Their lonely statistics speak for themselves. They are 500 times more likely to be single than their parents were, and even half of those who marry will probably divorce."[25] Churches that pursue boomers and busters must have a robust network of small-group ministries to enfold people into the church community. Three factors provide the rationale for this program.

Small Groups Are Biblical

Small groups were an integral part of the early church and vital to its life. In contrast to the typical American churches of the twentieth century, the various churches in the first century A.D. were rather large in size (Acts 1:13–15; 2:41; 4:4; 5:14, 15; 6:1; 9:31; 11:21, 24; 14:1, 21; 16:5; 17:4, 12; 18:8, 10; 19:26; 21:20). This presented a problem for the church. How could it minister personally and effectively to all these people? The church solved the problem by structuring their meetings around large and small groups (figure 14). The large-group meetings were used for evangelism (Acts 4:4; 5:42) and teaching and preaching (Acts 20:20). The small-group meetings met people's personal needs (Acts 2:44–45; 4:32–37) and as communities for the Lord's supper and worship (Acts 2:46), evangelism (Acts 5:42), prayer (Acts 12:12), and encouragement (Acts 16:40).

178

Figure 14

Acts 2:46   Acts 5:42   Acts 20:20

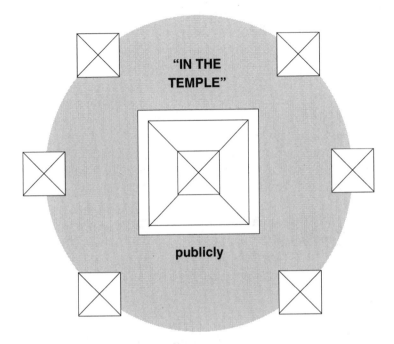

"HOUSE TO HOUSE"

Small Groups Facilitate Life Change

Most traditional churches are under the mistaken assumption that God uses the pastor's Sunday sermon as the primary vehicle for the transformation of people's lives. If this is the case, then God's plan has been largely frustrated. For example, most people can count on the fingers of one hand the number of sermons that have accomplished significant change in their lives.

While expository preaching is most important and contributes to life change, small-group ministry best facilitates the transformation of lives. When mature saints are asked what has contributed most to their growth in Christ, they usually refer to a significant relationship with one or more Christians. The obvious conclusion is that churches which take seriously the Great Commission mandate will implement a robust network of small groups.

Small Groups Prove Advantageous

Small groups provide solutions to various problems of ministry. One advantage is that they are not limited by facilities. They can meet practically anywhere—indoors or out-of-doors. Another is that they are geographically expandable. They can locate almost anywhere, whether next door to the church facility or on the opposite side of town. A third is that they encourage vital, personal relationships. People find it difficult to get to know one another in the typical Sunday morning worship service. If the dynamic is right, the small group solves this problem. A fourth is that small groups encourage lay ministry in that they provide a warm, non-threatening environment for the exercise of natural talents and spiritual gifts. A fifth is that they are not limited by finances. If there is any cost for operating a small-groups ministry, it is minimal. A sixth is that small groups decentralize pastoral care. The people who make up the group take care of their own. A seventh is that they facilitate leadership training. A well-designed program places an apprentice leader in each group who gains valuable on-the-job training in preparation to lead another group in the future. Finally, small groups promote the assimilation process. They provide believers with the necessary community that prevents them from slipping out the "back door" of the church.

Conclusion

The question was raised in the introduction to this book, Can you pour new wine into old wineskins? In Matthew 9:16–17, the Savior uses two illustrations (sewing a new patch of cloth on an old garment and pouring new wine into an old wineskin) to say you cannot. Some apply this passage to older, plateaued and declining churches and conclude that they cannot be revitalized. While there are a number of revitalized, growing churches across America, the existence of only one is enough to question the validity of this application.

The customs and circumstances surrounding Matthew 9:16–17 are important. The Pharisees fasted twice a week but had turned this practice into a display of outward piety. John's disciples were fasting in mourning over his death. In response to the question from the latter, Jesus compares himself to a bridegroom and teaches that it would be silly for his attendants (the disciples) to mourn (fast) while he is present. A wedding is a festive occasion, not a time for mourning. They can wait until he is gone to mourn—a cryptic allusion to the cross.

Jesus teaches that his way and the way of John's disciples and the Pharisees are unmixable. The contrast is between two antithetical systems, law and grace (John 1:17). This does not mean that people cannot change, because some Pharisees accepted Jesus as Messiah (Acts 15:5). It does mean that certain systems cannot be mixed, much like oil and water. One of the reasons why so many churches struggle at the end of the twentieth century is because their ways or systems no longer work. They performed well in the 1940s and 1950s but are antithetical to the ways of the 1990s. But just as John's disciples and Pharisees can change and adopt new systems, so people in struggling churches can follow suit.

In light of the difficult circumstances of 80 to 85 percent of North American churches at the end of the twentieth century, the hope for the future of the church is change. More specifically, this hope focuses on change through two primary areas of ministry: church birth and church revitalization.[1] The future of the church in North America is dependent on them. This book is based on the concept that people can and will change and is dedicated to equipping leaders for this task.

Worksheets

Change

1. What fundamental changes, in addition to those listed by Joel Arthur Barker, can you identify that have taken place in the last twenty years? Barker wrote *Discovering the Future* in 1985. What changes have taken place since then?

2. What are some recent effects of change on Americans' lives that you have noticed? How has change affected you personally within the last few years?

3. What are some of the fads and trends of newer churches across America? Can you identify the paradigms behind them? Describe them. Are you attracted to any of them? Why?

4. Are you a paradigm shifter? Are you willing to take risks and develop a new set of rules for your present ministry? If not, have you contemplated a move to a new ministry?

5. Have you ever experienced a paradigm shift in ministry? If yes, what did you see that was different after the shift? Are there people around you who reject new paradigms? Do you understand why they do this? What, if anything, will you do about it?

Megachange

1. In your opinion, what is the current state of the mainline churches in your community—growing, plateaued, or in decline? On what do you base this opinion (personal observation, published data, conversations with knowledgeable people, other)?

2. What is the current state of the evangelical churches in your community—growing, plateaued, or in decline? On what do you base your opinion?

3. Examine your church's worship attendance over the past few years. Is your church plateaued, or in decline? Why?

4. Are any churches in your community growing? Is their growth from transfer, from conversion, or biological?

5. What percentage of the population in your community is unchurched? What percentage of these unchurched people are preboomers, baby boomers, or baby busters?

6. Do you believe these unchurched people can be reached with the gospel of Christ? Can they be reached through the ministry of your church? Why or why not?

7. What would your church have to change to reach the unchurched? Is it willing to make these changes? Are you willing to make them?

Divine Design

1. Read through the spiritual qualifications for leadership in 1 Timothy 3 and Titus 1. Do you meet the qualifications for spiritual leadership? Why or why not? If your answer is no, which qualifications do you not meet, and what do you plan to do about it?

2. List below your spiritual gifts. Is one a primary gift around which the others cluster? If so, list it first.

    a.

    b.

    c.

    d.

    e.

3. Do any of your gifts match those which, according to chapter 3, are characteristic of change agents? Write them down. Is this true of your primary gift?

4. What is your passion? Do you have a deep, gut feeling toward a particular ministry? Is it the established, typical church?

5. What is your temperament according to the *Personal Profile/Biblical Personal Profile*? Circle the appropriate letter below.

    Primary: D   i   S   C

    Secondary: D   i   S   C

How close is your profile to the persuader profile? Does it fall within the range in Thomas's operational profile?

6. What is your temperament according to the *Myers-Briggs Type Indicator (MBTI)?* Circle the appropriate preferences below.

E	I
S	N
T	F
J	P

How does your profile compare with that discussed in chapter 3?

7. List your natural characteristics and abilities. Ask someone who knows you well to do the same. How does your list compare with Nehemiah's characteristics and abilities? It is not necessary that you have all of Nehemiah's. Which ones do you have and which ones do you not have? Which does your current situation call for?

8. Based on the information above, do you believe that God has designed you to be a pastor who leads churches through change? If not, has he designed you to work under such a person?

Resistance to Change

1. Write out the specific changes you are attempting to implement in your ministry.

2. What kind of resistance to these changes do you encounter? Which of the twelve reasons listed below might explain this resistance?

Felt needs

Status quo

Values

Vested interests

Distrust of leadership

The stress of change

Differences of temperament

Sacred cows

The complexity of change

The paradigm effect

Ethnocentrism

Self-centeredness

Other reasons

3. How might the solutions to each of these reasons suggested in chapter 5 apply to your situation?

People of Change

1. Estimate the percentage of people in your church who fall within each of the four categories of change response. Write the percentages on the lines below. Which category has the largest percentage of people?

Early adopters_____   Middle adopters_____

Early innovators_____   Late adopters_____

Early adapters_____   Never adopters_____

2. Having completed exercise 1, evaluate each layer of opinion makers in your church in terms of whether they are predominantly early, middle, late, or never adopters. Assign them both a percentage and a grade from A to F. Place that percentage and grade beside each layer and write any helpful comments in the circles on p. 189.

3. What conclusions, based on exercises 1 and 2, would you draw about possible changes in your church?

4. In light of the information gained in exercises 1 and 2 and question 3, should you attempt to introduce change in this church?

5. According to chapter 6, how might you implement change on each layer of opinion makers?

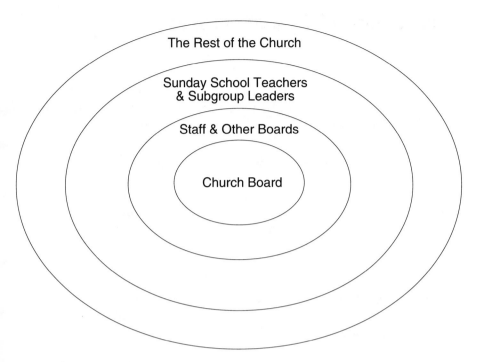

The Rest of the Church

Sunday School Teachers
& Subgroup Leaders

Staff & Other Boards

Church Board

Windows of Opportunities

1. Is your church experiencing a crisis, or has it experienced some crises recently? Identify it or them. How might you use this seeming difficulty to bring needed change to your ministry?

2. Are you thinking about leaving your church? Why? Have you been there longer than five to eight years? Could your thoughts be premature? Do you need to experience personal renewal? Do you regularly expose yourself to new paradigm ideas (books, tapes, and so on), or have you attended a good pastors' conference within the last year? What can you do right now to correct this problem?

3. Have you recently moved to a different church? Is the new church plateaued or in decline? How might you use this situation to initiate a new direction for the church? Should you move quickly or slowly? Why?

4. Has your church ever planted another church? Why not? Are these reasons valid or simply excuses not to change? (Most fall in the latter category—really!).

5. Have you or has the church ever used the expertise of a consultant? Why, or why not? How might a consultant be of help in your present situation? If you are in a denominational church, does the denomination offer consultation?

6. Have you and your board ever attended a cutting-edge pastors' conference together? Why not? What would it take for this to happen? How might you encourage your board to accompany you? Would it be worth going, even if all the board cannot attend? Would it be worth your time if only one or two board members caught your vision?

7. Is your church in a serious decline? Is death fairly certain? Would it be wise for you to close the church and use this as an opportunity to bring new life out of the old situation? What is stopping you?

190

How to Change

1. Approximately how much time do you spend in prayer each day? How much of this time do you take to pray for change in the church?

2. Is your church plateaued or in decline? How do you know? What might this condition tell you about the timing of the change process?

3. What are some of the reasons why your church maintains the status quo? What are some of the signs that God is directly intervening in the church's life? What are some direct means you can implement to encourage discontent with the status quo?

4. Can you articulate a powerful, significant vision for your ministry? What is it? Does it challenge people as well as give them ministry direction? What are some of the ways you plan to communicate this vision? How often?

5. Once you have a clear, succinct vision, develop a plan to implement that vision. What are some of the elements that will appear in the plan?

6. Are you convinced of the importance of team ministry? Who will be on your team? Are they early, middle, late, or never adopters? Who are the early adopters in the church? Who in the congregation has come after your arrival and is younger than you? Are they early adopters?

7. How do you plan to keep the congregation from slipping back to their old ways once change has been implemented?

Change Principles

1. Would the Savior be impressed with your faith? Why, or why not? Could your faith be described as an "easy" or a "tough" faith? Can you find any parallels between the circumstances surrounding Noah's and Abraham's and your faith?

2. In your conversations with people in your ministry, do you offer ultimatums or ask insightful questions? What are some of the changes needed in your ministry? What questions could you ask to promote these changes?

3. Do the people under your leadership react negatively to the use of the word *change?* What other terms might you adopt that are less inflammatory? Write them down and intentionally begin to use them.

4. How would you rate your ministry's ability to communicate: good, average, or poor? How would you rate your own ability to communicate? Are you a good listener (you might want to ask your spouse or a close friend)? What are some of the opportunities in your ministry to communicate more directly with your people? Do you give the people periodic progress reports? Have you ever leaked any information? Do you communicate positively or negatively? (Ask several people in your congregation whom you respect for their honesty.)

5. What role does the governing board play in the decision-making process in your church? Are its members advocates of the status quo or of meaningful, significant change? Have you ever established an ad hoc committee? Why or why not? Who might serve well on such future committees?

6. How would you characterize the changes you are attempting to make: addition, subtraction, or replacement? Are you in a plateaued or a declining situation? Which is the best kind of change for your situation? Why?

7. At what level is the majority of change that takes place in your ministry: compliance, identification, or internalization? What percentage would you assign to each level? What does this tell you about the quality of change in your church?

A New Face for the Church

1. If you have developed a vision statement for your ministry, ask the following questions: Is it clear? Is it challenging? Is it a picture of the future of your ministry? Do you believe that it *can be*? Are you convinced that it *must be*?

2. Is your vision essentially the Great Commission? Does your ministry pursue lost people? How? Are you reaching lost people? What is the evidence? Do you disciple saved people? How? Is your ministry balanced between pursuing and evangelizing lost people and discipling Christians?

3. Do you consider yourself a leader? Are you a godly person? What do you do to develop your character? How often? What is your personal and organizational vision? Does the vision for your present ministry (organizational vision) match your personal-ministry vision? If not, what do you plan to do about it? Do you have any followers? Who are they? Why are they following you?

4. Do you consider yourself to be a strong leader? Do others? Are you a leader of leaders or "another one of the boys"? Are you a servant leader? What is the evidence of your servanthood?

5. What percentage of your congregation is mobilized for service and what percentage is not? Are you satisfied with these figures? Why are not more people involved in ministry in your church? What do you plan to do about it?

6. Would the Pepsi generation describe your church as a dinosaur? Take a sheet of paper and write *biblical functions* as the heading on the upper left side and *cultural forms* on the upper right. Place the church's functions and forms under the appropriate heading. Were you able to separate the functions from the forms? What did you learn? Where would you make some changes?

7. Would you describe your worship as authentic or inauthentic? Why? What is the church's attitude toward the importance of worship? Have you experienced authentic, holistic worship? What happened? Visit several churches in the area that are known for their worship styles. Which style best fits your ministry? How might you implement this kind of worship in your church?

8. Are you satisfied with the evangelism efforts in your church? Why or why not? If not, what are some of the reasons why the church is not more evangelistic? When your people hear the term *evangelism*, what style of evangelism do they think of first? Why? What styles of evangelism are evident in your church? What could you do to help people discover, develop, and practice their unique styles of evangelism?

9. Does your ministry have an active network of small groups? If so, would you describe them as robust? Why or why not? Do you depend on God to use your preaching to produce life change? Is it happening? Why or why not?

Suggestions for Further Reading

Anderson, Leith. *A Church for the Twenty-first Century*. Minneapolis, Minn.: Bethany House Publishers, 1992.

_____. *Dying for Change*. Minneapolis, Minn.: Bethany House Publishers, 1990.

Arn, Win. *The Pastor's Manual for Effective Ministry*. Monrovia, Calif.: Church Growth, Inc., 1988.

Barker, Joel Arthur. *Future Edge: Discovering the New Paradigms of Success*. New York: William Morrow and Company, Inc., 1992.

Barna, George. *The Frog in the Kettle*. Ventura, Calif.: Regal Books, 1990.

_____. *User Friendly Churches*. Ventura, Calif.: Regal Books, 1991.

Callahan, Kennon L. *Effective Church Leadership*. San Francisco: Harper & Row, Publishers, 1990.

Carroll, Jackson W., Douglas W. Johnson, and Martin E. Marty. *Religion in America: 1950 to the Present*. San Francisco: Harper & Row, Publishers, 1979.

Dickson, Elaine. *Say No, Say Yes to Change*. Nashville: Broadman Press, 1982.

Ellis, Joe S. *The Church on Purpose*. Cincinnati: Standard Publishing, 1982.

Gallup, George. *The Unchurched American—10 Years Later*. Princeton, N.J.: The Princeton Religion Center, 1988.

Geier, John G., and Dorothy E. Downey. *Personal Profile System*. Minneapolis, Minn.: Performax Systems International, Inc., 1977.

George, Carl F. *Prepare Your Church for the Future*. New York: Fleming H. Revell Company, 1991.

Gerber, Michael E. *The E-Myth*. New York: Harper Business, 1986.

Griffin, Em. *The Mind Changers*. Wheaton: Tyndale House Publishers, Inc., 1976.

Hadaway, C. Kirk. *Church Growth Principles*. Nashville: Broadman Press, 1991.

Hunter, George G. *How to Reach Secular People*. Nashville: Abingdon Press, 1992.

Keirsey, David, and Marilyn Bates. *Please Understand Me*. Del Mar, Calif.: Promethean, 1978.

Kotter, John P. *A Force for Change*. New York: The Free Press, 1990.

Kouzes, James M., and Barry Z. Posner. *The Leadership Challenge*. San Francisco: Jossey-Bass Publishers, 1987.

Malphurs, Aubrey M. *Developing a Vision for Ministry in the Twenty-first Century*. Grand Rapids: Baker Book House, 1992.

_____. *Planting Growing Churches for the Twenty-first Century*. Grand Rapids: Baker Book House, 1992.

Naisbitt, John, and Patricia Aburdene. *Megatrends 2000*. New York: William Morrow and Company, Inc., 1990.

Oswald, Roy M., and Otto Kroeger. *Personality Type and Religious Leadership*. Washington, D.C.: The Alban Institute, 1988.

Peters, Tom. *Thriving on Chaos*. New York: Harper & Row, Publishers, 1987.

Sanders, J. Oswald. *Spiritual Leadership*. Chicago: Moody Press, 1980.

Schaller, Lyle E. *Create Your Own Future!* Nashville: Abingdon Press, 1991.

_____. *The Change Agent*. Nashville: Abingdon Press, 1972.

_____. *44 Questions for Church Planters*. Nashville: Abingdon Press, 1991.

_____. *Activating the Passive Church*. Nashville: Abingdon Press, 1981.

_____. *Getting Things Done*. Nashville: Abingdon Press, 1986.

Thomas, Robert W. *Personality Characteristics of Effective Revitalization Pastors in Small, Passive Baptist General Conference Churches*. D. Min. Dissertation, Talbot School of Theology, 1989.

Tucker, Robert B. *Managing the Future*. New York: Berkley Books, 1991.

Voges, Ken, and Ron Braund. *Understanding How Others Misunderstand You*. Chicago: Moody Press, 1991.

Wagner, C. Peter. *Church Planting for a Greater Harvest*. Ventura, Calif.: Regal Books, 1990.

_____. *Leading Your Church to Growth*. Ventura, Calif.: Regal Books, 1984.

Walrath, Douglas A. *Leading Churches Through Change*. Nashville: Abingdon Press, 1979.

Notes

Introduction

1. Win Arn, *The Pastor's Manual for Effective Ministry* (Monrovia, Calif.: Church Growth, Inc., 1988), p. 16.

2. "Church Planting: A Bold New Approach to Evangelism in the 90s," *Ministry,* Summer 1991, p. 2.

3. Lyle E. Schaller, *Create Your Own Future!* (Nashville: Abingdon Press, 1991), p. 111.

4. Haddon Robinson, *Compass* (2010 Sybil Lane, Tyler, TX 75703) Volume 2, Issue 2.

5. See my book entitled *Planting Growing Churches for the Twenty-first Century* (Grand Rapids: Baker Book House, 1992).

6. Ralph Neighbour, Jr., *Where Do We Go from Here?* (Houston: Touch Publications, Inc., 1990), p. 92.

7. Lyle E. Schaller, *The Change Agent* (Nashville: Abingdon, 1972), p. 11.

8. George Barna, *User Friendly Churches* (Ventura, Calif.: Regal Books, 1991), p. 22.

Chapter 1: Megachange and America

1. Tom Peters uses the stronger words *loving change* rather than *living for change.* He writes, "Today, loving change, tumult, even chaos is a prerequisite for survival, let alone success." Tom Peters, *Thriving on Chaos* (New York: Harper & Row, Publishers, 1987), p. 56.

2. Michael E. Gerber, *The E-Myth* (New York: Harper Business, 1986), p. 156.

3. Pat Baldwin, "Forecasting the '90s," *The Dallas Morning News,* October 27, 1991, 1J.

4. George Barna, *The Frog in the Kettle* (Ventura, Calif.: Regal Books, 1990), p. 49.

5. Gerber, *The E-Myth,* p. 157.

6. Robert B. Tucker, *Managing the Future* (New York: Berkley Books, 1991), p. 11.

7. Joel Arthur Barker, *Discovering the Future* (St. Paul, Minn.: ILI Press, 1985), pp. 3, 6.

8. Tom Peters, *Thriving on Chaos* (New York: Harper & Row, Publishers, 1987), p. 55.

9. Joel Arthur Barker, *Future Edge: Discovering the New Paradigms of Success* (New York: William Morrow and Company, Inc., 1992), pp. 22–24.

10. Gerber, *The E-Myth*, p. 156.

11. Barker, *Discovering the Future*, pp. 2–3.

12. Tucker, *Managing the Future*, pp. 9–10.

13. John Naisbitt and Patricia Aburdene, *Megatrends 2000* (New York: William Morrow and Company, Inc., 1990), p. 11.

14. Ibid., p. 12.

15. Barker, *Discovering the Future*, p. 14.

16. Ibid., p. 15.

17. Ibid., p. 42.

Chapter 2: Megachange and the Church

1. Leith Anderson has written *Dying for Change* (Minneapolis, Minn.: Bethany House Publishers, 1990). I have used the title of his excellent book as the title for this chapter.

2. C. Kirk Hadaway, *Church Growth Principles* (Nashville: Broadman Press, 1991), p. 110.

3. Win Arn, *The Pastor's Manual for Effective Ministry* (Monrovia, Calif.: Church Growth, Inc., 1988), p. 41.

4. Ibid., p. 43.

5. Ibid.

6. Wade Clark Roof and William McKinney, *American Mainline Religion: Its Changing Shape and Future* (New Brunswick, N.J.: Rutgers University Press, 1987), p. 6.

7. Constant H. Jacquet, Jr., ed., *Yearbook of American and Canadian Churches, 1988* (Nashville: Abingdon Press, 1988), p. 263. I have rounded the figures.

8. Roof and McKinney, *American Mainline Religion*, p. 6.

9. Jacquet, *Yearbook*, p. 263. I have rounded the figures.

10. "Missions Memo," *Missions USA*, July–August 1988, p. 2.

11. Helen Parmley, "Adding Up Membership," *The Dallas Morning News*, October 19, 1991, 38A.

12. C. Peter Wagner, *Church Planting for a Greater Harvest* (Ventura, Calif.: Regal Books, 1990), p. 14.

13. Lyle Schaller, *44 Questions for Church Planters* (Nashville: Abingdon Press, 1991), p. 20.

14. Jackson W. Carroll, Douglas W. Johnson, and Martin E. Marty, *Religion in America: 1950 to the Present* (San Francisco: Harper & Row, Publishers, 1979), p. 16.

15. See James Hunter, *Evangelism: The Coming Generation* (Chicago: University of Chicago Press, 1987), pp. 203–7.

16. Lyle E. Schaller, *Create Your Own Future!* (Nashville: Abingdon Press, 1991), p. 111.

17. Arn, *The Pastor's Manual for Effective Ministry*, p. 16.

18. "Church Planting: A Bold New Approach to Evangelism in the 90s," *Ministry*, Summer 1991, p. 2.

19. "Churches Die with Dignity," *Christianity Today,* January 14, 1991, p. 70.

20. Ibid., p. 69.

21. Gary L. McIntosh, "Baby Busters," *The McIntosh Growth Network,* August 1990, p. 1.

22. Ibid.

23. George G. Hunter, III, *How to Reach Secular People* (Nashville: Abingdon Press, 1992), p. 41.

24. Judy Howard, "Back in the Fold," *The Dallas Morning News,* May 25, 1991, 41A.

25. George Gallup, *The Unchurched American—10 Years Later* (Princeton, N.J.: The Princeton Religion Center, 1988), p. 2.

26. Ibid.

27. Ibid.

28. Ibid.

29. "Church Growth Fine Tunes Its Formula," *Christianity Today,* June 24, 1991, pp. 46–47.

30. Hunter, *How to Reach Secular People,* p. 24.

31. *Leadership,* Spring 1992, p. 133.

32. George Barna, *The Frog in the Kettle* (Ventura, Calif.: Regal Books, 1990), p. 142.

33. Gallup, *The Unchurched American—10 Years Later,* p. 3.

34. Barna, *The Frog in the Kettle,* p. 119.

35. Jack Sims, "Baby Boomers: Time to Pass the Torch?" *Christian Life,* January 1986, p. 24.

36. Ibid.

37. George Barna, "The Case of the Missing Boomers," *Ministry Currents,* January–March 1992, Volume II, Number 1, p. 2.

38. Ibid.

39. Ibid.

40. David Briggs, "Study: Ex-Protestants Not Returning to Fold," *The Dallas Morning News,* June 5, 1992, 6A.

41. Ibid.

42. Ibid.

43. Jeffrey L. Sheler with Betsy Wagner, "Latter-day Struggles," *U.S. News & World Report,* September 28, 1992, p. 73.

44. Jacquet, *Yearbook of American and Canadian Churches 1990,* p. 262.

45. John Naisbitt and Patricia Aburdene, *Megatrends 2000* (New York: William Morrow and Company, Inc., 1990), p. 270.

46. Sheler and Wagner, *Time,* p. 74.

47. Jacquet, *Yearbook of American and Canadian Churches 1990,* p. 262.

48. Naisbitt and Aburdene, *Megatrends 2000,* p. 280.

49. George Barna, *The Frog in the Kettle* (Ventura, Calif.: Regal Books, 1990), p. 141.

Chapter 3: The Preparation for Assessment

1. I have described the area of assessment in greater detail in *Planting Growing Churches for the Twenty-first Century* (Grand Rapids: Baker Book House, 1992), chaps. 5–6. I also intend to write a book on this topic in the next few years.

2. Lyle E. Schaller, *Activating the Passive Church* (Nashville: Abingdon Press, 1981), p. 11.

3. Source unknown.

4. Charles C. Ryrie, *The Holy Spirit* (Chicago: Moody Press, 1965), p. 83.

5. The Charles E. Fuller Institute provides several different gifts inventories. Their address is P.O. Box 90910, Pasadena, CA 91109-0910.

6. This material on gift mix and gift cluster and the terms have been influenced by Robert Clinton's *The Making of a Leader* (Colorado Springs, Colo.: Navpress, 1988).

7. You may also order the *Personal Profile* from the Charles E. Fuller Institute or write to the Carlson Learning Company, P.O. Box 1763, Minneapolis, MN 55440-9238.

8. Ken Voges and Ron Braund, *Understanding How Others Misunderstand You* (Chicago: Moody Press, 1991), p. 39.

9. This assessment is not available for use by the general public but can be taken through a professional counseling center or a consulting agency. However, a modified form of it is *The Keirsey Temperament Sorter*, which is in the book *Please Understand Me* (Del Mar, Calif.: Promethean, 1978) written by David Keirsey and Marilyn Bates. You can order it from Prometheus Nemesis Book Company, Box 2748, Del Mar, CA 92014. The phone number is (619) 632-1575 and cost is only $11.95. The obvious advantage of ordering the book is the cost and the full explanations of the various types.

10. James M. Kouzes and Barry Z. Posner, *The Leadership Challenge* (San Francisco: Jossey-Bass Publishers, 1987), pp. 284–90.

11. Lyle E. Schaller, "Megachurch!" *Christianity Today*, March 5, 1990, pp. 22–23.

Chapter 4: The Practice of Assessment

1. In a personal conversation Lyle Schaller stated that he believes *who* is more important than *how*.

2. The scriptural evidence for this is presented in chapter 10 in the discussion of the strong servant-pastor. The concept is developed more fully in Aubrey Malphurs, *Planting Growing Churches for the Twenty-first Century* (Grand Rapids: Baker Book House, 1992).

3. J. Oswald Sanders, *Spiritual Leadership* (Chicago: Moody Press, 1980), p. 51.

4. Ibid., p. 52.

5. Ibid.

6. Ibid., pp. 52–53.

7. Ibid., p. 53.

8. Ibid.

9. Ibid., p. 55.

10. Ibid.

11. Ibid., p. 56.

12. Ibid., p. 57.

13. Ibid., p. 58.

14. Ibid., p. 59.

15. The NIV uses the term *herald* rather than *preacher.*

16. Lyle E. Schaller, *Create Your Own Future!* (Nashville: Abingdon Press, 1991), pp. 24–25.

17. C. Peter Wagner, *Leading Your Church to Growth* (Ventura, Calif.: Regal Books, 1984), p. 97.

18. The *Personal Profile* and the *Biblical Personal Profile* essentially are the same. The difference is that the latter explains and compares the various temperaments to those of Bible characters.

19. This sample population seems rather low. Thomas acknowledges this as a potential weakness in that he was not able to include the total population of successful Baptist General Conference revitalization pastors in the project. However, he concludes that the statistics of the project reflect a number close to the total population and, therefore, reflect a high degree of reliability.

20. John G. Geier and Dorothy E. Downey, *Personal Profile System* (Minneapolis, Minn.: Performax Systems International, 1977), p. 17.

21. Ibid.

22. Ken R. Voges, *Workbook: Level I Part A.* The Biblical Behavioral Series, (Minneapolis, Minn.: Performax Systems International, 1986), p. 6.

23. Robert W. Thomas, "Personality Characteristics of Effective Revitalization Pastors in Small, Passive Baptist General Conference Churches," (D. Min. dissertation, Talbot School of Theology, 1989), p. 102.

24. Roy M. Oswald and Otto Kroeger, *Personality Type and Religious Leadership* (Washington, D.C.: The Alban Institute, 1988), p. 30.

25. Ibid., p. 69.

26. Ibid., p. 68.

27. Ibid., p. 41.

28. Ibid., p. 81.

29. Ibid., p. 41.

30. Ibid., p. 65.

31. Joel Arthur Barker, *Discovering the Future* (St. Paul, Minn.: ILI Press, 1989), p. 35.

32. Ibid., p. 25.

33. Ibid., pp. 26–27.

34. Ibid., p. 27.

35. Lyle E. Schaller, *Create Your Own Future!* (Nashville: Abingdon Press, 1991), pp. 24–25.

36. Barker, *Discoverimg the Future*, p. 37.

Chapter 5: Why People Don't Change

1. Kennon L. Callahan, *Effective Church Leadership* (San Francisco: Harper & Row, Publishers, 1990), p. 4.

2. Lyle E. Schaller, *Getting Things Done* (Nashville: Abingdon Press, 1986), p. 152.

3. Ibid.

4. This is my conclusion after conducting a survey of the Division of Ministries at Dallas Theological Seminary.

5. Pastor Gary Inrig has influenced my thinking in this area. See his article "Between Trapezes," *Interest,* March 1987, Volume 53, Number 1, p. 11.

6. Schaller, *Getting Things Done,* p. 153.

7. Joel Arthur Barker, *Discovering the Future* (St. Paul, Minn.: ILI Press, 1989), p. 90.

8. Ibid.

9. George Barna, *The Frog in the Kettle* (Ventura, Calif.: Regal Books, 1990), p. 49.

10. Ibid., p. 31.

11. Kenneth O. Gangel, *Feeding & Leading* (Wheaton, Ill.: Victor Books, 1989), p. 149.

12. Ken R. Voges, *Biblical Personal Profile* (Minneapolis, Minn.: Performax Systems International, 1985), p. 7.

13. Ibid.

14. David Keirsey and Marilyn Bates, *Please Understand Me: Character and Temperament Types* (Del Mar, Calif.: Prometheus Nemesis Book Company, 1978), p. 47.

15. Ibid., pp. 154–55.

16. Ibid., p. 155. Also, Roy M. Oswald and Otto Kroeger, *Personality Type and Religious Leadership* (New York: The Alban Institute, Inc., 1988), p. 23.

17. Keirsey and Bates, *Please Understand Me,* p. 155.

18. Ibid.

19. Ibid., p. 153.

20. Keirsey and Bates, *Please Understand Me,* p. 155; and Oswald and Kroeger, *Personality Type and Religious Leadership,* p. 23.

21. Keirsey and Bates, *Please Understand Me,* p. 154.

22. The DiSC can be ordered from the Charles E. Fuller Institute, P.O. Box 90910, Pasadena, CA 91109-0910. Their phone number is (800) CFULLER. For information regarding DiSC qualification training write the Carlson Learning Company, Training Division, P.O. Box 59159, Minneapolis, MN 55439-8247 or call (612) 449-2868.

23. For information on MBTI training write to the Center for Applications of Psychological Type, Inc., 2720 N.W. 6th Street, Gainesville, FL 32609 or call them at (904) 375-0160.

24. You can order *Please Understand Me* from Prometheus Nemesis Book Company, Box 2748, Del Mar, CA 92014. Phone (619) 632-1575.

25. Elaine Dickson, *Say No, Say Yes to Change* (Nashville: Broadman Press, 1982), p. 84.

26. John P. Kotter writes about the concepts of leadership and management and how they relate to one another in terms of change and complexity in *A Force for Change: How Leadership Differs from Management* (New York: The Free Press, 1990).

27. Barker, *Discovering the Future,* p. 42.

28. Ibid.

29. Ibid.

30. Contact Charthouse Learning Corporation for more information. Their toll-free number is (800) 328-3789 or you may write them at Charthouse Learning Corporation, 221 River Ridge Circle, Burnsville, MN 55337.

31. The concept of crisis and change will be explored further in chapter 7.

Chapter 6: The People of Change

1. Win Arn, *The Pastor's Manual for Effective Ministry* (Monrovia, Calif.: Church Growth, Inc., 1988), p. 50.
2. John G. Geier and Dorothy E. Downey, *Personal Profile System* (Minneapolis, Minn.: Performax Systems International, 1977), p. 15.
3. Joe S. Ellis, *The Church on Purpose* (Cincinnati: Standard Publishing, 1982), p. 179.
4. Geier and Downey, *Personal Profile*, p. 7.
5. Ibid.
6. Ellis, *The Church on Purpose*, p. 179.
7. Lyle E. Schaller, *Create Your Own Future* (Nashville: Abingdon Press, 1991), p. 25.
8. Ibid., p. 43.
9. Ellis, *The Church on Purpose*, p. 180.
10. Arn, *The Pastor's Manual for Effective Ministry*, p. 50.
11. Ibid.
12. Ibid.
13. Leith Anderson, *Dying for Change* (Minneapolis: Bethany House Publishers, 1990), p. 178.
14. Ibid., p. 177.
15. Ibid.
16. The wisdom of this approach to church leadership is coming into question as leaders consider new paradigms for ministry in the twenty-first century. Except for the church, few organizations would ever operate this way. An alternative view is presented in chapter 10.
17. Anderson, *Dying for Change*, p. 178.
18. Ibid.
19. Ibid.
20. Ibid.
21. Ibid.
22. Ibid.
23. Ibid.

Chapter 7: The Times for Change

1. Win Arn, *The Pastor's Manual for Effective Ministry* (Monrovia, Calif.: Church Growth, Inc., 1988), p. 43.
2. Ibid.
3. Lloyd M. Perry and Edward J. Lias, *A Manual for Pastoral Problems and Procedures* (Grand Rapids: Baker Book House, 1962), p. 39.
4. Terry Muck, *When to Take a Risk* (Carol Stream, Ill.: Word Books, 1987), p. 127.
5. Lyle E. Schaller, *Create Your Own Future!* (Nashville: Abingdon Press, 1991), p. 75.
6. Robert W. Thomas, "Personality Characteristics of Effective Revitalization Pastors in Small, Passive Baptist General Conference Churches," (D. Min. dissertation, Talbot School of Theology, 1989), p. 4.
7. Schaller, *Create Your Own Future!* p. 73.

8. Carl F. George, *Prepare Your Church for the Future* (New York: Fleming H. Revell Company, 1991), p. 46.

9. C. Kirk Hadaway, *Church Growth Principles* (Nashville: Broadman Press, 1991), p. 101.

10. Lyle E. Schaller, *Hey, That's Our Church* (Nashville: Abingdon Press, 1975), p. 96.

11. C. Kirk Hadaway, *Church Growth Principles* (Nashville: Broadman Press, 1991), p. 76.

12. Win Arn, "Pastoral Tenure and Church Growth," *The Win Arn Growth Report*, Pasadena, California, Volume 1, Number 36.

13. Hadaway, *Church Growth Principles*, p. 77.

14. Ibid., p. 105.

15. C. Peter Wagner, *Your Church Can Grow* (Ventura, Calif.: Regal Books, 1984), p. 61.

16. Dean Merrill, "Mothering a New Church," *Leadership*, Winter 1985, p. 105.

17. Ibid.

18. "Churches Die With Dignity," *Christianity Today*, January 14, 1991, p. 70.

19. Arn, *Pastor's Manual for Effective Ministry*, p. 44.

20. Write both the Charles E. Fuller Institute of Evangelism and Church Growth, P.O. Box 90910, Pasadena, CA 91109-0910 and Church Growth 2000, 1921 So. Myrtle Avenue, Monrovia, CA 91016 for a catalog of the most current books and tapes.

21. Arn, *The Pastor's Manual for Effective Ministry*, p. 43.

22. Ibid.

23. Ibid.

24. Ibid.

Chapter 8: The Process of Change

1. Lyle E. Schaller, *Create Your Own Future!* (Nashville: Abingdon Press, 1991), p. 75.

2. Sherri Brown, "The Search for Saddleback Sam," *Missions USA*, July–August, 1988, p. 18.

3. Lyle E. Schaller, *The Change Agent* (Nashville: Abingdon Press, 1972), p. 86.

4. Em Griffin, *The Mind Changers* (Wheaton: Tyndale House Publishers, Inc., 1976), pp. 3–9.

5. Schaller, *The Change Agent*, p. 89.

6. Ibid., p. 90.

7. For a complete treatment of the concept of organizational vision see Aubrey Malphurs, *Developing a Vision for Ministry in the Twenty-first Century* (Grand Rapids: Baker Book House, 1992).

8. Ibid., chap. 1.

9. Ibid., p. 31.

10. For a detailed discussion of these methods and others see Aubrey Malphurs, *Developing a Vision for Ministry in the Twenty-first Century* (Grand Rapids: Baker Book House, 1992), chap. 5.

11. C. Kirk Hadaway, *Church Growth Principles* (Nashville: Broadman Press, 1991), p. 83.

12. James M. Kouzes and Barry Z. Posner, *The Leadership Challenge* (San Francisco: Jossey-Bass Publishers, 1987), p. 233.

13. Elaine Dickson, *Say No, Say Yes to Change* (Nashville: Broadman Press, 1982), p. 26.

14. Robert W. Thomas, "Personality Characteristics of Effective Revitalization Pastors in Small, Passive Baptist General Conference Churches," (D. Min. dissertation, Talbot School of Theology, 1989), p. 4.

15. Ibid., p. 5.

16. The purpose of this chapter is not to explore all the facets of planning. There are a number of good books designed specifically for this purpose. The ingredients of a good ministry plan and a sample for a planted church are found in Malphurs, *Developing a Vision for the Twenty-first Century*, chap. 8.

17. Thomas, "Personality Characteristics of Effective Revitalization Pastors in Small, Passive Baptist General Conference Churches," pp.4–5.

18. Ibid., p. 80.

19. Hadaway, *Church Growth Principles*, pp. 83–84.

20. Thomas, "Personality Characteristics of Effective Revitalization Pastors in Small, Passive Baptist General Conference Churches," p. 33.

21. Lyle E. Schaller, *The Change Agent* (Nashville: Abingdon Press, 1972), p. 117.

Chapter 9: The Tools of Change

1. Dallas Willard, *The Spirit of the Disciplines* (San Francisco: Harper & Row, Publishers, 1988), p. 184.

2. Ibid., p. 186.

3. James M. Kouzes and Barry Z. Posner, *The Leadership Challenge* (San Francisco: Jossey-Bass Publishers, 1987), p. 52.

4. Elaine Dickson, *Say No, Say Yes to Change* (Nashville: Broadman Press, 1982), p. 24.

5. Ibid., pp. 23–24.

6. Albert H. Morehead, gen. ed., *The New American Roget's College Thesaurus in Dictionary Form* (New York: The New American Library, Inc., 1962), p. 50.

7. Joe S. Ellis, *The Church on Purpose* (Cincinnati: Standard Publishing, 1982), pp. 182–83.

8. Lyle E. Schaller, *Growing Plans* (Nashville: Abingdon Press, 1983), p. 48.

9. Gary L. McIntosh, *The McIntosh Church Growth Network* (3630 Camellia Drive, San Bernardino, CA 92404) Volume 2, Number 6.

10. Lyle E. Schaller, *Create Your Own Future!* (Nashville: Abingdon Press, 1991), p. 135.

11. Ibid., p. 25.

12. Ibid., p. 22.

13. Ibid., p. 31.

14. Ibid., p. 73.

15. Ibid., p. 74.

16. Elaine Dickson, *Say No, Say Yes to Change* (Nashville: Broadman Press, 1982), p. 52.

17. Ibid., p. 54.

18. Ibid.

19. Ibid., p. 55.
20. Ibid., p. 56.

Chapter 10: The Future Church

1. In addition, see Luke 5:27–32 and 15:1–10.
2. Walter L. Liefeld, *Luke*, Vol. 8 of *The Expositor's Bible Commentary*, ed. Frank E. Gaebelein (Grand Rapids: Zondervan Publishing House, 1984), p. 1008.
3. Kennon L. Callahan, *Effective Church Leadership* (San Francisco: Harper & Row, Publishers, 1990), p. 13.
4. Ibid. p. 8.
5. George Gallup, Jr., *The Unchurched American—10 Years Later* (Princeton, N.J.: The Princeton Research Center, 1988), p. 4.
6. Callahan, *Effective Church Leadership*, p. 26.
7. This section is developed further in Aubrey Malphurs, *Planting Growing Churches for the Twenty-first Century* (Grand Rapids: Baker Book House, 1992), chap. 8.
8. Ibid., chap. 9.
9. Some pastors and churches would take strong exception to this. They argue that pastors are not leading well because they do not know how. They would lay some of the blame at the feet of the seminaries and colleges who do not stress leadership development and place too much value on classroom education over field training.
10. I would disagree that it is a good form for small churches if those churches want to grow.
11. C. Peter Wagner, *Leading Your Church to Growth* (Ventura, Calif.: Regal Books, 1984), p. 119.
12. J. Oswald Sanders, *Spiritual Leadership* (Chicago: Moody Press, 1980), p. 27.
13. Ibid., pp. 27–30.
14. Win Arn, "Pastoral Tenure and Church Growth," *The Win Arn Growth Report*, Pasadena, California, Volume 1, Number 36.
15. Frank Tillapaugh, *Unleashing the Church* (Ventura, Calif.: Regal Books, 1982), p. 20.
16. I highly recommend the *Networking* program developed by Bruce Bugbee of Willow Creek Community Church near Chicago. This program has influenced my thinking in this area. It can be ordered from the Charles E. Fuller Institute, P.O. Box 91990, Pasadena, CA 91109-1990.
17. I recommend the *Personal Profile* (DiSC), marketed by the Carlson Learning Company. This temperament tool and several spiritual gifts inventories can also be ordered from the Charles E. Fuller Institute.
18. Ronald Allen and Gordon Borror, *Worship* (Portland, Oreg.: Multnomah Press, 1982), pp. 67–68.
19. Ibid., p. 9.
20. This does not mean that the traditional service does not need to change. If it is to remain vibrant, it must experience incremental change.
21. Floyd Bartel, *A New Look at Church Growth* (Newton, Kans: Faith & Life Press, 1987), p. 59.

22. George Barna, *The Frog in the Kettle* (Ventura, Calif.: Regal Books, 1990), p. 115.

23. Bill Hybels, *Honest to God?* (Grand Rapids: Zondervan Publishing House, 1990), pp. 126–32.

24. Paula Rinehart, "The Pivotal Generation," *Christianity Today,* October 6, 1989, p. 24.

25. Ibid.

Conclusion

1. I have written a book on church planting: *Planting Growing Churches for the Twenty-first Century* (Grand Rapids: Baker Book House, 1992).

Index

Abilities, natural, 53, 70–76
Administration, gift of, 62
Aging, 115
Aldrich, Joe, 176
Allen, Ronald, 172–73
Anderson, Leith, 27, 106, 109, 110,
Arn, Win, 13, 28, 32, 33, 105, 114,
    122, 124, 125, 167
Assemblies of God, 29, 31, 32
Assessment, organizational value of,
    46–48; practice of, 57–76; purpose
    of, 48–56; self-assessment, 44–46;
    value of, 44–48
Attendance. *See* Church, decline in

Baby boom generation, 13, 33–34,
    36–37, 86, 121, 124, 178, 184
Baby bust generation, 33–34, 124, 184
Baptist General Conference, 64
Barker, Joel Arthur, 20, 22, 23–24, 25,
    71, 73–74, 85, 94, 183
Barna, George, 13, 14, 15, 20, 35, 36,
    38, 87, 176
Bartel, Floyd, 176
Bates, Marilyn, 70, 91
Bear Valley Baptist Church, 15
Biblical gifts, 51
Biblical Personal Profile, 64, 66, 73, 91,
    185
Boards, church, 107–9, 122, 192
Borror, Gordon, 172–73
Buddhism, 38
Building program, 123

Callahan, Kennon, 82, 161
Carroll, Jackson, 31
Carter, Gary, 120–21
Change, advantages of, 132; anticipat-
    ing, 23–26; by compliance, 153,
    192; by identification, 154, 192; by
    internalization, 154, 192; commit-
    tees for, 150–51; communication
    for, 148–50; complexity of, 93;
    developing a plan of, 135–38;
    impact of, 22–23; kinds of, 20–22.
    151–53, 192; levels of, 133–39,
    153–55; need for, 79–81; process
    of, 127–41, 143, 144; questions of,
    146–47; resistance, 79–97, 187;
    response to, 100–6; sacredness of
    resistance to, 91–92; statistics of,
    19–20; stress of, 87–88; terms of,
    147–48; time for, 113–25; threat of,
    132
Charles E. Fuller Institute of
    Evangelism and Church Growth,
    119
Christian and Missionary Alliance, 29,
    31, 32
Church Growth, Inc., 119
Church, boards, 107–9, 122, 192;
    closing, 130, decline of, 25, 28–32,
    33, 63, 115, 119, 121, 131, 152,
    181, 184, 190, 191, 192; death of,
    32–33, 48, 128; image in commu-
    nity, 131; plateau of, 33, 48, 63, 80,
    114, 117, 118, 119, 128, 131, 151,

209